"Discovery has provided our groups with the very best arrangements for travel to Israel and points beyond. We have never been disappointed and con- sider it a privilege to share with our people the experience of a lifetime. Discovery makes it happen with class and a heart-filled commitment to ministry.
—Dr. Jack Graham, Prestonwood Church, Plano, Texas

"Integrity...Honesty...Experience. These words best describe Discovery. Want the best? Travel with Discovery."
—Dr. O.S. Hawkins, President, GuideStone Investments of the Southern Baptist Convention

"Discovery excels in planning and leading tours to Israel. They are among the very best."
—Dr. Johnny Hunt, First Baptist Church, Woodstock, Georgia

"Discovery is not a travel business...it is indeed a Christian ministry. The folks with Discovery have a love for the Lord and Israel that is contagious...a call to minister by helping others discover the marvelous land of the Bible. They know the country, they know the people, they know how to lead you and your church on the trip of a lifetime. For many years Discovery has led the Second Baptist Church of Houston, and the Winning Walk Ministry through the land of the Bible. Remember, Discovery is not a business...it is a ministry...it is personal. Their knowledge of His land is surpassed only by their love and heart for Him."
—Dr. Ed Young, Second Baptist Church, Houston, Texas

"Discovery has made our trips to Israel seamless while handling every detail with courtesy and professionalism. No organization does it better. I highly recommend Victor Frazier and his team to all my friends. Why not travel with the Best?"
—Dr. James MacDonald, Harvest Bible Church, Chicago, Illinois

D0112188

WALKING WHERE JESUS WALKED

A Traveler's Guide to Ancient Israel

GARY FRAZIER

Discovery Cruises and Tours

Published for Discovery Cruises and Tours
PO Box 2148
Hurst, Texas 76053
www.discoveryworldwideministries.com

Cover and interior design by David Daniels

First Printing 2017

Unless otherwise indicated, Scripture is taken from the Holy Bible, *New
International Version*®, Copyright © 1984, 2001, 2010 by Biblica, Inc.™

CONTENTS

Your Tour Day-By-Day

ABOUT THE AUTHOR

Gary Frazier is a respected author and speaker on Bible prophecy and current events, speaking in churches and conferences regularly. He is a former pastor and has traveled to Israel more than 100 times since the 70's.

Gary currently serves in an advisory capacity with Discovery Cruises and Tours, one of America's leading group tour specialists whose mission is to educate and equip Christ followers concerning Israel's right to exist as well as their role in Biblical prophecy. In addition, Gary founded *Discovery Missions International* in 1985 and serves as its President as well as the Executive Vice-President of *United in Purpose*, a non-profit cultural change organization working to turn America back to God.

Gary's educational background includes Criswell College, South- western Seminary and he holds both an M.A. and a Ph.D. from Louisiana Baptist University. Gary has been honored with a Doctor of Humanities degree from Liberty University as well as a Doctor of Divinity degree from International Seminary.

Gary has appeared on numerous documentaries such as the History Channel's *God vs. Satan* and *The Apocalypse Code*. He has also appeared regularly on *Prophecy in the News, The King is Coming, Trinity Broadcasting,* DayStar TV, *Christ in Prophecy, The King is Coming, Point of View* radio, Moody and Salem radio networks.

He has authored 14 books including *Miracle of Israel, It Could Happen Tomorrow, Hell is for Real, Signs of the Coming of Christ, The Divine Appointment* and *What Happens When You Die,* as well as numerous DVD and CD teaching series. He also contributed to the *LaHaye Prophecy Study Bible* and *The Prophecy Encyclopedia*.

Gary is a commercial, multi-engine rated pilot and an avid golfer. Gary and Sandra, with four grown children and eight grandchildren, reside in the Dallas/Ft. Worth Metro area. Connect with Gary :

email@garyfrazier.com   www,garyfrazier.com

817.715.0840   817.595.270

TWITTER: @garyfrazier7   **FACEBOOK:** DrGaryFrazier

WELCOME!

Dear Holy Land Traveler,

The material in this day-by-day guide to His Land represents the result of more than 40 years and more than 150 trips to Israel, personal study of the Word of God and many, many resource materials and literally hundreds of hours spent with the most knowledgeable guides in The Land.

We know firsthand your life will never be the same once you experience The Land of our Lord Jesus Christ. While it is true we do not have to come to Israel to find Christ, it is also true His presence is very real to the believer who seeks to know Him better, not just to know more about Him.

It is our prayerful desire you will use this guide to enrich your days in His Land. Furthermore upon your return from The Land, this new found knowledge will give you a deeper love for Him, His Word and His People.

Until HE Comes,
Discovery Cruises and Tours

PREPARING FOR YOUR TOUR

Some people are seasoned travelers. Others are starting a new adventure. The following instructions are provided to help make your Holy Land Tour most memorable.

PACKING

Do not pack valuables. Carry with you or leave them at home.

One suitcase per person. Storage space is *very limited* on the tour bus. We allow one piece of luggage (50 lbs. max). Do not confuse this with any carry-on luggage (40 lbs. max) you may take with you. Leave room in your luggage for anything you might buy to bring home and/or pack a small fold-up suitcase for your purchases.

Dress casual. Clothes should be comfortable and modest. Mix-and-match and layered outfits work well. All shorts should come to the knee. Shorts are forbidden at some holy sites, so you may want to wear more slacks than shorts. If you choose to wear a sleeveless top, you will need to have a cover-up available for some locations. Also, you may want to bring a bathing suit and water shoes as there will be opportunities to swim. A waterproof jacket with zip out lining and/or sweater may be desired during some seasons of travel.

For evening dinner, women may want to bring something a little dressier as we will be staying in some very nice hotels. Men will *not* be expected to have a sport coat; however, you may want at least one nice shirt for evening wear.

Wear comfortable, nonskid shoes. We will be doing a lot of walking on uneven terrain, so prepare accordingly.

11

Watch out for sunburn. The sun can be quite warm, so a hat or small umbrella may be desirable as well as sunglasses and sunscreen. If using an umbrella, please be aware of other travelers around you so that they can see the tour guide and sites.

Electrical appliances requirements. Electric current in Israel is 220 volts and the plug is different. You can get an assortment of international plug adapters and converters at Wal-Mart, Container Store, Amazon, etc. Check the maximum number of watts of the appliance you may be using. Curling irons should work on either 220 or 110 current. Hair dryers are available in the hotels.

Keep your passport or airline ticket with you. Always keep your ticket and passport accessible in your carry-on. Never pack them in your checked baggage. Make a photocopy of your passport to carry with you and a copy to leave at home.

Other things to consider. You may wish to pack washcloths; hand wipe wash-n-dries for warm touring days; your own soap, if important to you; and/or travel detergent. Each day, the hotel desk will ring a wake-up call, but you may want to carry your own alarm clock.

TIPS FOR AIR AND BUS TRAVEL

One carry-on per person. Your carry-on baggage must fit under the seat in front of you or in the airline overhead compartment. Keep this carry-on small because we are limited in bus space. Travelers are also allowed to carry a purse or small backpack.

Keep important items in your carry-on. Keep your valuables, such as cameras, phone, power cords, passport, etc., with you in your carry-on. Also keep medicines (in their original containers or with a prescription copy), make-up, toothbrush, and eye glasses with you.

Extra travel items. Frequent travelers know that there are some things which help make long-haul trips more comfortable:

> Hand sanitizer	> Pens/highlighters
> Inflatable neck pillow	> Breath mints
> Eye shades	> Toothbrush/Paste
> Sturdy, refillable water bottle	> Warm socks
> Candy bars/granola bars	> Headphones

WHILE IN ISRAEL

Shopping. English is spoken everywhere in Israel so that no language problem need arise. Shopping is fun, but be careful with your money. Street peddlers and shops sometimes overcharge for things of little worth. Don't feel pressured to buy. Part of the fun in shopping is the Middle Eastern culture of "bargaining" for an item. When bargaining with a peddler, never accept the first price of an item as the actual price. Usually the item can be purchased for about half of the "asking price." Keep a record of all your purchases, this will make the filing of your customs report easier. Keep small amounts of money accessible so that you don't have to pull out all of your money in a public place.

Money belts. A money belt is suggested. There are some pickpockets in Israel, so make sure you have a purse that closes securely or a safe way to carry your money and passport. Do not carry an open purse and/or make sure your backpack is secured with a clip.

Currency. You may use American dollars in Israel. Smaller denominations are best. One-dollar bills come in very handy ($100-$150 per person). Some may wish to bring $300-$500 in cash for shopping. However, U.S. checks and credit cards are accepted in most gift shops. Keep cash, traveler's checks, and passport on your person, *not in your suitcase or hotel room.* Larger purchases can be made using a major credit card, but go through your wallet or purse before leaving the United States to remove all unnecessary credit cards (just in case your wallet is lost or stolen). Make a copy of the credit cards you take with you. Notify credit card companies of the dates you will be traveling.

Water. Drink plenty of fluids while in Israel. While the water is generally safe, bottled water is widely available and high recommended. As an added convenience, bottled water is normally available for you on the bus for a nominal fee ($1).

Bibles. It is recommended that you bring a small Bible with you and this Tour Study Guide for making notes of each site you visit.

Laundry. You may wish to do hand laundry in your bathroom (bring your own detergent). Hotels laundry service is expensive and is an additional charge to you if you wish to use it.

Traveling as part of a group. A large group has to work together to stay together. Please keep up with the group and don't wander off on your own excursion as you will force the rest of the group to wait for you. Please return to the bus at times stated by your Tour Guide so that the tour may continue on time and your group visit as many sites as possible each day. As with any trip, expect some minor inconveniences such as schedule changes. Flexibility is the key!

Weather. The temperatures in Israel vary and we recommend checking the web and weather stations in advance of your trip. The Internet provides forecast anywhere from 10 days to 2 weeks. You will want to pack accordingly and layering is suggested. December through April you may encounter rain. However rain is highly unlikely during the remaining months and should it rain it will be brief. The chart below will provide examples of typical temps

	March	May	June	July
Tel Aviv	51-69	63-77	67-83	70-86
Sea of Galilee	51-72	62-89	68-95	73-98
Jerusalem	44-61	60-77	63-81	66-84
Dead Sea	61-78	75-93	80-99	81-102

OVERCOMING JET LAG

The time difference between Central Standard Time in the USA and Israel is +8 hours. That is, when it is noon in DFW, it is 8 pm in Jerusalem. Your body may take a couple of days to adjust to jet lag. The following principles are intended to help you adjust your "body clock" to the new time schedule:

Three days before your trip: Stop consuming any beverage or foods containing caffeine until the day of the flight.

Two days before departure: Fast. Try to limit your total calorie intake to 800 calories if possible. Eat a high protein breakfast and lunch and a high carbohydrate supper. Do not have any snacks after dinner. No caffeine.

One day before departure: Feast. Allow yourself generous portions at meals, but do not snack after dinner. No caffeine. Again eat a high protein breakfast and lunch, and a high carbohydrate evening meal.

Day of Departure. Arise earlier than usual. This is a fast day. Try to limit your calorie intake to 800 calories. Eat a high protein breakfast and lunch. The evening meal will be served on the transatlantic portion of your flight. Drink a lot of water or decaffeinated beverages to compensate for the dehydration that is common to long flights. Set your wristwatch ahead to the destination time. Try to rest or sleep as soon as possible on the flight. When not resting or sleeping, walk around the plane aisles periodically to get some exercise to minimize the swelling of your legs and feet.

First day of arrival. Eat a good breakfast and drink some black coffee, strong plain tea or caffeinated soft drinks. Avoid caffeine the rest of the day. Feast during the day. Keep active. Go to bed by 10 pm. Your body should be almost adjusted to the change in time zones. Eat well, keep active, don't allow yourself to nap, and enjoy your time in Israel.

FLIGHT SECURITY AND CONNECTIONS

For security reasons, never take any mail or packages to hand deliver to anyone when you get to Israel. Security is **very tight** and you will be interrogated very carefully. Answer all questions honestly and politely. **Do not** upset immigration officers. Also **do not** embellish your answers...answer **only** the questions asked.

Carry a copy of your passport, separate from the passport itself. Also, it is suggested that you carry small bills for easy access and separate from your other money.

TOUR SCHEDULE

Discovery Cruises and Tours wants your tour to be the trip of a lifetime and will work with local guides to insure that your group visits as many sites as possible. In some cases, weather, special events in Israel or group delays will prevent a group from visiting a particular site or may require the tour to visit sites in an order not reflected in this guide.

שָׁלוֹם

SPEAKING HEBREW

You will not need to know any Hebrew to enjoy every aspect of your tour. However, you might wish to try out a few Hebrew words as you immerse yourself in the beautiful culture of Israel.

Hello (Peace)	*shalom (shah-LOHM)*
Bye (Peace)	*shalom (shah-LOHM)*
Good morning	*boker tov (BOH-ker TOHV)*
Good afternoon	*tsohorayim tovim*
	(tsoh-hoh-RAH-yeem toh-VEEM)
Good evening	*`erev tov (EH-rev TOHV)*
Good night	*laylah tov (LIGH-lah TOHV)*
How are you? (M)	*mah shlomkha? (mah shlom-KHAH)*
How are you? (F)	*mah shlomekh? (mah shloh-MEKH)*
How are you?	*mah nishma[`]? (mah nish-MAH)*
What's up?	*mah koreh? (mah kor-EH)*
Thank you	*todah (toh-DAH)*
Please/ You're welcome	*bevakashah (be-vah-kuh-SHAH)*
Excuse me. (Forgiveness)	*slihah (slee-KHAH)*
What is your name? (said to a M)	*ma shimkha*
What is your name? (said to a F)	*ma shmekh*
My name Isaiah..	*shmi*
How much is it?	*kamah zeh (KA-mah zeh)*

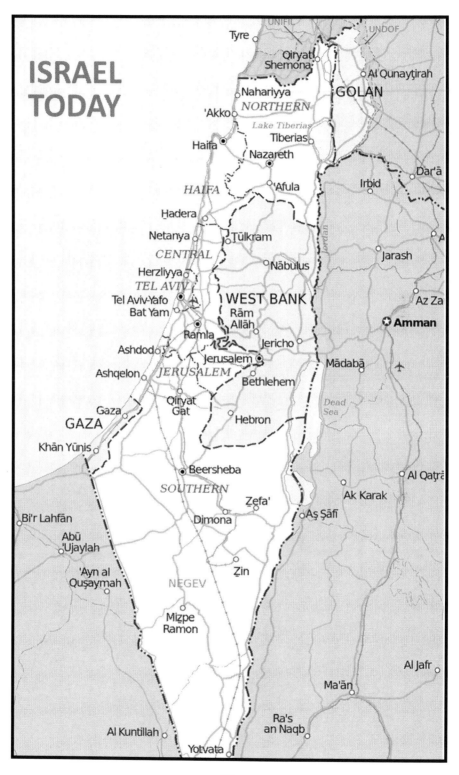

ISRAEL
TODAY

Tyre

Qiryat
Shemona

Al Qunayṭirah

Nahariyya   GOLAN

NORTHERN

'Akko

Lake Tiberias

Haifa   Tiberias

Nazareth

HAIFA   'Afula   Irbid

Dar'ā

Ḥadera

Netanya   Tūlkram

CENTRAL   Jarash

Herzliyya   Nābulus

TEL AVIV

Tel Aviv-Yafo   WEST BANK   Az Za

Bat Yam   Rām
                   Allāh
                                                   Amman

Ramla
                         Jericho

Ashdod

Jerusalem   Mādabā

Ashqelon   JERUSALEM

Bethlehem

Qiryat
Gat   Dead
                                   Sea

Gaza   Hebron

GAZA

Khān Yūnis

Beersheba   Al Qaṭrā

SOUTHERN

Zefa'   Ak Karak

Bi'r Lahfān   Dimona   Aṣ Ṣāfī

Abū
Ujaylah

'Ayn al   Zin
Quṣaymah   NEGEV

Miẓpe
Ramon

Al Jafr

Ma'ān

Al Kuntillah   Ra's
                 an Naqb

Yotvata

17

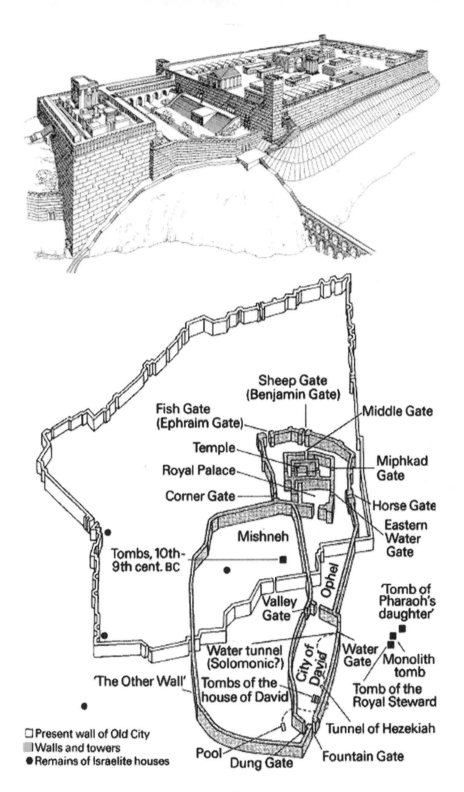

Sheep Gate
(Benjamin Gate)

Fish Gate
(Ephraim Gate)

Middle Gate

Temple

Miphkad
Gate

Royal Palace

Corner Gate

Horse Gate

Eastern
Water
Gate

Mishneh

Tombs, 10th–
9th cent. BC

Ophel

'Tomb of
Pharaoh's
daughter'

Valley
Gate

Water
Gate

Monolith
tomb

Water tunnel
(Solomonic?)

City of David

'The Other Wall'

Tombs of the
house of David

Tomb of the
Royal Steward

Tunnel of Hezekiah

☐ Present wall of Old City
▨ Walls and towers
● Remains of Israelite houses

Pool

Dung Gate

Fountain Gate

A BRIEF HISTORY OF THE HOLY LAND

The prophet Isaiah asked the question, *"Can a country be born in a day or a nation brought forth in a moment? Yet, no sooner is Zion in labor than she gives birth to her children"* (Isaiah 66:8). And so it was, on the 14th of May 1948, in direct fulfillment of this prophecy and countless others, after having been scattered into the four corners of the earth since 70 A.D., the nation of Israel was birthed! God did a new thing! Some- thing that has never happened before! No nation, in the history of the world, has lost its identity, been scattered and absorbed into other civilizations and then re-emerged after nearly 2000 years as a distinct and individual people once again! The people of Israel have **returned** to their land, **revived** their ancient language and are seeing the **restoration** of their land! Do miracles really happen in today's world? One only need look at Israel to know the answer is, Yes!

Modern Israel is surrounded by Muslim countries on three sides and the Mediterranean Sea to the west. She is bounded on the north by Lebanon, on the east by Syria and Jordan and on the south by Egypt. She is further surrounded by a total of 20 Arab countries and, while each of these countries is struggling under various forms of oppression, Israel is surging ahead as the only democratic society in the Middle East.

Pre-Biblical Period   4000—2000 B.C.
The oldest known communities on Earth were in the Holy Land.

Biblical Period — Beginning with Abraham, 2160 B.C.

In about 2160-2100 B.C., Abraham arrived in Canaan. Originally he had departed from Ur of Chaldea near the Persian Gulf in what is today Iraq; and after a few years in Haran, north of Canaan, he arrived in the land under the leadership of God.

Ca 1445	Moses leads the children of God out from 400 years of Egyptian bondage.
Ca 1400	Joshua enters the Promised Land.
Ca 1200	Philistines from Crete invade Israel and occupy five principal cities along the Mediterranean coast: Ashdod, Ashkelon, Gath, Gaza and Ekron.
1025	Saul was crowned as Israel's first king.
1004-965	David reigns as King of Israel.
965-922	Solomon reigns as King of Israel and builds the First Temple in Jerusalem on the site of the threshing floor of Araunah the Jebusite, which had been purchased by his father, King David (II Samuel 24:18ff).
Ca 920	Israel is divided into the northern and southern kingdoms at the death of Solomon: Israel in the north, with its capital at Samaria, consisting of 10 tribes and Judah in the south, with its capital in Jerusalem, consisting of only Judah and Benjamin.
722	Assyria captures the 10 tribes of the Northern Kingdom and takes them captive to the north and they are lost to history.

Babylonian Period — 605—562 B.C.

605	Nebuchadnezzar lays siege to Jerusalem and takes away captives to Babylon. Daniel the prophet is in this first group of captives.
586	Nebuchadnezzar attacks Jerusalem and this time destroys the Temple of Solomon, carries away the treasures of the Temple, and takes Judah captive to Babylon.

Persian Period — 549—332 B.C.

536	Cyrus allows the Jews to return to Jerusalem exactly 70 years after their captivity as prophesied by Jeremiah and Daniel.
445	Artaxerses issues the decree to restore and rebuild Jerusalem. This is the beginning of Daniel's 70 weeks of prophecy in Daniel 9:25ff.

Greek Period 332—167 B.C.

332	Alexander the Great conquers Israel. Upon his death, his kingdom is divided into fourths, and Israel is ruled by the Ptolemy's of Egypt.
197	Israel passes into the hands of the Seleucid Empire when Antiochus III defeats the Egyptians at Caesarea Philippi.
175	Antiochus IV (Epiphanies) of Syria becomes king.
167	Antiochus abolishes worship of Jehovah and desecrates the second Temple in Jerusalem by offering a swine on the Temple altar and in-stalling a statue of the Olympian Zeus.

Hasmonean Period 167—63 B.C.

In response to the atrocities of Antiochus, the Jews revolt under the leadership of the Maccabaean brothers and overthrow the Seleucids. The Jews now have about 100 years of self-rule under their own leaders known as the Hasmoneans. It was during this period that two opposing groups sprang up, the Pharisees and Sadducees.

Roman Period 63 B.C.—330 A.D.

63 B.C.	Pompey conquers Israel for Rome.
40 B.C.	The Parthians surprise the Romans under the leadership of Antigonus and took the land.
39 B.C.	Herod the Great expels the Parthians and the Romans are once again in command. Herod is rewarded by Rome and becomes the King of the Jews and reigns until his death in 4 B.C.
4-1 B.C.	In this time period, Jesus was born in Bethlehem.
32 A.D.	Jesus was crucified in Jerusalem.
66 A.D.	This is the year of the first Jewish revolt which started in Caesarea led by the Zealots.
70 A.D.	In response to the Jewish revolt, Titus destroys the Temple and the city of Jerusalem is burned. The Jewish people are scattered in what is known as the *Great Diaspora* or *Scattering* into the four corners of the earth and for nearly 2,000 years there is no Israel.
132 A.D.	The Jews who remained in the land revolt against the Romans a second time under the leadership of Bar Kokhba, and once again are further scattered and badly defeated.

135 A.D.	The Roman Emperor Hadrian rebuilds Jerusa-lem as a Roman and much smaller city. He moves the line of the walls on the southern side to their present location and changes the name of Jerusalem to Aelia Capitolina. He changes Judea to Syria Pales-tina, Syria of the Philistines and hence, the name Palestine (Isa. 14:29, 31). He also issues a decree that no Jew can ap-proach the city under penalty of death.

Byzantine Period   312—634 A.D.

Constantine becomes the Roman Emperor in 312. He has a vision during a battle in which he sees a cross in the sky and the words, "in this sign conquer." He becomes a Christian and declares the Roman Empire *Christianized*, which brings persecution and suffering to an end, but also moves Christianity from being people-oriented to build-ing- and institution-oriented. Pagan priests now become Christian priests and the living church is infiltrated with people whose hearts have not been changed by the power of the living Lord Jesus Christ. The Christian religion spreads rapidly through-out the Roman world which eventually leads to the Roman Catholic or Universal Church birthed in the early 5th century. This also brings a split in the empire and Constantinople, Istanbul of today, becomes the capital of the east-ern half of the Roman Empire.

2nd Persian Period   607—629 A.D.

While things in Europe were changing, so was Israel. On May 20, 614, Jerusalem was overrun by the Persians, Christian churches were destroyed, and the work of about 300 years of con-struction was al-most wiped out. The Church of the Holy Sepulcher in Jerusalem was destroyed, while the Church of the Nativity in Bethlehem was miracu-lously spared.

Arab Period   634—1099 A.D.

570	Mohammed is born in Mecca. When he is 43, he receives a se-ries of revelations, which later becomes the *Koran*, the "Bible" of the Moslems. In 632 he dies; however, in this short period of 19 years, he is able to weld the Arab tribes together with this new religion.

636	After the death of Mohammed, a split occurs between his leadership and two branches of Islam develop, the Shiites and the Sunnites or Sunnis. As a result of this split, Jerusalem becomes the third holiest city in Islam, next to Mecca and Medina in Saudi Arabia of today.
1009	Fatimid Caliph Hakim issues the order to destroy the Church of the Holy Sepulcher again, and this began the destruction of 30,000 Christian buildings in Israel. This action was the spark that set off the Crusades.

Crusader Period   1099-1263 A.D.

1099	The Crusaders from Europe arrive in Israel and Jerusalem is captured from the Moslems. This is the beginning of the Latin Kingdom of Jerusalem.
1187	A Moslem prince named Saladin from Egypt gains control of Egypt, Syria, Mesopotamia and Israel (or Palestine) and defeats the Crusaders in a strategic battle at the Horns of Hittin in Galilee. The battles rage and the Christians gain control for a short period of 13 years before losing once again to Mongol tribes from central Asia in the early 13th century.

Mameluke Period   1263—1516 A.D

1263	The Mamelukes of Egypt capture the few remaining Crusader strongholds along the coast and hold them intermittently for the next 250 years.

Turkish Period   1517—1917 A.D

1517	The Ottoman Turkish Empire, which was birthed after the breakup of the great Mongol Empire of Genghis Khan, spread into the Middle East in the early years of the 16th century and held the land for 400 years while reigning from Constantinople. The Turks cut all the trees in the Holy Land and used them to build railroads, etc., throughout their empire.
1799	Napoleon tries to add Palestine to his kingdom but fails at Acre.
1917	Under the leadership of the British General Allenby, a devoted Christian, Jerusalem is liberated by the Allies at the end of World War I.

1878	The first of the early pioneers return to the land and establish a village at Petah Tikvah.
1909	The first Kibbutz in the land is founded at the southern tip of the Sea of Galilee and named Degania.
1917	The land is liberated from the Turks. The Balfour Declaration, proclaiming the need for a Jewish homeland in so-called Palestine, is announced by the British Lord Balfour. This is a very important day as it signals the soon return to the land of the Jewish people in large numbers. Between the years 1917-1944, many Jews try to return to the land but they are limited by quotas placed by the British who are afraid of the Moslems. Because of this, millions die in Nazi concentration camps.
1922	The British Mandate over Palestine is confirmed by the League of Nations.
1947	The League of Nations offers the Moslem Palestinians an opportunity to have a state of their own alongside Israel, but they refuse. This leads to a Partition Plan between Israel and Jordan that is adopted by the United Nations.
1948	On May 14, the State of Israel was re-born in fulfillment of Biblical Prophecy, and the British withdraw. This is the beginning of the Jewish War of Independence. The war officially ends July 18 and Israel is established on a small portion of their land; however, they do not have possession of Jerusalem, Judea or Samaria. This land is now known as Trans Jordan and is under the control of the Jordanians.
1949	David Ben-Gurion becomes the first Prime Minister of Israel. He is a Zionist and an atheist.
1956	Israel fights with Egypt after the Egyptians, led by Gamal Abdul Nasser, nationalize the Suez Canal in July. In October, the Israelis end up occupying nearly all of the Sinai Peninsula. After peace terms are agreed upon, Israel pulls back to the 1949 armistice lines and U.N. forces are stationed along the Israeli-Egyptian border.
1967	On May 23, Egypt closes the Gulf of Aqaba to Israeli shipping, and on June 5, the famous Six Day War breaks out. After just six days, the Israelis liberate Samaria and Judea (so-called West Bank) by pushing the Syrians out of the Golan Heights in the north, the Jordanians from Jerusalem across the Jordan River to the east, and the Egyptians out of the Sinai to the south. For the first time since 70 A.D. the Jews have control of Jerusalem and now have access to the Wailing Wall.

1969	Golda Meir becomes Israel's fourth Prime Minister.
1970-73	Israel fights a War of Attrition in the Jordan Valley against the Jordanians.
1973	On October 6, the holiest day of the Jewish year, Yom Kippur (Day of Atonement), Israel is attacked by Syria and Egypt. Israel holds its territory and is victorious but not without the loss of many young Jewish lives.
1979	On March 26, Egyptian President Anwar Sadat and Israeli Prime Minister Menachem Begin sign a peace treaty in Washington D.C. Later, Mr. Sadat is assassinated by Moslem fundamentalists.
1982	In response to continued missile attacks from Lebanon, Israel enters southern Lebanon on June 5, and establishes a security belt between Lebanon and Israel.
1985	Israel annexes the Golan Heights.
1986	The Arab Moslem Intifada breaks out and Israel begins a campaign of containment.
1994	Israel agrees to give up land for peace and enters into an agreement with Yasser Arafat and the PLO which gives the PLO control of Gaza and Jericho.
1995	Israel plans negotiations with Syria that will result in the giving up of the Golan Heights which leads to widespread dissension among Israelis. On November 4, Prime Minister Yitshak Rabin is assassinated and becomes the first Prime Minister in Jewish history to be killed by one of his own. In December, Israel gives over control of Bethlehem and Nablus to the PLO.
1996	Benjamin Netanyahu is elected Prime Minister, replacing Shimon Peres. Israel pulls out of Hebron as part of the treaties. The population of Israel is 5.9 million.
1997	Israel and the Palestinians reach agreement on Israeli redeployment in the West-Bank city of Hebron and the Hebron Protocol is signed by Israel and the Palestinian Authority.
2001	Ariel Sharon is elected Prime Minister and Israel withdraws from the Gaza Strip.
2002	The "Quartet" (United States, European Union, Russia and United Nations) proposes the Road Map for Peace to resolve Israeli-Palestinians conflict and create an independent Palestinian state. The Israeli army launches Operation Defensive Shield on West Bank after several Palestinian suicide bombings. This was the largest military operation on West Bank since 1967.

2003	Israel and the Palestinian Authority accept the Road Map for Peace, which requires a freeze on the West Bank Jewish settlements and an end to attacks on Israelis. A right-of-center coalition government is formed by Prime Minister Ariel Sharon.
2005	Israel carries out the Disengagement Plan, ending Israel's presence in the Gaza Strip. Israel withdraws all Jewish settlers and military personnel from Gaza, while retaining control over airspace, coastal waters and border crossings.
2006	Ehud Olmert becomes acting Prime Minister. Israeli incursion into Lebanon, in response to deadly Hezbollah attack and abduction of two soldiers escalates into the Second Lebanon War. Shimon Peres is elected President by the Knesset.
2007	The Palestinian Unity Agreement (Mecca Agreement) is signed in Mecca. The Annapolis Conference establishes, for the first time, a "two-state solution" as the basis for future talks between Israel and the Palestinian Authority.
2008	Arabs threaten to withdraw its proposed Arab peace Initiative if Israel does not accept it. Israel launches its Gaza Operation (Operation Cast Lead) in response to the barrage of more than 10,000 rockets and mortars fired from the Gaza Strip.
2009	Benjamin Netanyahu is elected Prime Minister. The population of Israel is 7.5 million and about 5.62 million are Jewish.
2013	Israel launches a week-long military campaign against Gaza-based armed groups following months of escalating rocket attacks on Israeli towns. Talks resume with the Palestinian Authority under U.S. auspices, but reach no conclusions. Israel, Jordan, and the Palestinian Authority sign an agreement to save the Dead Sea from drying up by pumping water from the Red Sea.
2014	Israel responds to attacks by armed groups in Gaza with a military campaign by air and land to knock out missile launching sites and attack tunnels. Clashes end in an uneasy Egyptian-brokered cease fire in August.
2015	Prime Minister Netanyahu forms a new coalition government after March elections with right-wing Bayit Yehudi (Jewish Home) party. Israel suspends contact with EU officials in talks with Palestinians over the EU decision to label goods from Jewish settlements in the West Bank as coming not from Israel but from settlements. Permanent members of the UN and Iran reach a controversial nuclear deal which Israel opposes.

2016	The U.S. agrees to a military aid package worth $38B over next 10 years for Israel, the largest such deal in U.S. history. Israel suspends working ties with 12 countries that voted for a Security Council resolution condemning settlement building after the U.S., for the first time, abstained from the vote rather than using its veto.
2017	President Trump and Netanyahu meet and announce U.S./Israel relations are reset. Trump denounces the Iranian nuclear deal and does not back a two-state solution. Israeli population exceeds 8 million.

NOTES

DAY 1

When you awake this morning, you may have to pinch yourself to believe you are really in *"The Promised Land"* . . . the Land of the Bible, the Land where Jesus walked! Stop just a moment and thank the Lord Jesus Christ for allowing you to make this journey. Multitudes of believers would love to be where you are this very day!

If you are changing hotels today, please put your checked luggage outside your door before coming to breakfast. If you have charged anything to your room, kindly clear your bill and leave your key at the front desk.

Following a delightful Israeli Sabra Breakfast Buffet, we begin our first day of touring. Now, on to the bus as we begin our spiritual and educational journey! Notice on the map you are given as you board the bus that we are on the coastal plain of the Mediterranean Sea, which is located on the western side of Israel. We will be traveling north and northeast as our day progresses.

CAESAREA

Caesarea is a seaport city situated on the Mediterranean approximately 30 miles north of the ancient port city of Joppa. Herod the Great began building Caesarea in 22 B.C. to accommodate his summer palace, and it took 12 years to complete. The city is built on the ancient site of Strato's Tower, and served as the capital of the Roman government in the land that was called Palestine for about 500 years (Israel should never be referred to as Palestine, as this name was derived from the land of the Philistines and is considered derogatory by the Israeli people). The city was named in honor of Caesar Augustus (Luke 2:1) and had lavish palaces, public buildings, a temple to Augustus, a theater, a hippo-drome, an amphitheater and an elaborate sewer system.

The harbor Herod built was considered a great architectural achievement, as it was protected from the waves of the sea by a massive breakwater which was built by letting down huge stones into the water, 20 fathoms deep.

Caesarea was the home of the Roman procurators who governed the land, including Pontius Pilate. In fact, as you enter the excavated ruins, you will see a replica of a stone discovered here which is the first archaeological evidence of Pontius Pilate's existence. It bears an inscription of the names of Emperor Tiberius (for which the Galilean city of Tiberias is named) and Pontius Pilate, who ruled from 26-36 A.D., and who sentenced Jesus Christ to crucifixion. In addition, Herod Agrippa the First died at Caesarea, having been eaten by worms (Acts 12:19-23).

Caesarea was the site of the beginning of the Jewish revolt in 66 A.D., which resulted in the destruction of Jerusalem in 70 A.D. and Masada in 73 A.D.

Not far north of the theater you will see the remains of a Crusader city with its dry moat (circa 1099). You will also see many crumbled Roman columns, as well as a Minaret from the Turkish occupation (1517-1917). You will also see a Roman Hippodrome that spans over 1,000 feet and accommodated 20,000 people in the ancient city, as well as a 1st-century aqueduct that supplied water to the city from the Mount Carmel Springs, some 12 miles away.

BIBLE REFERENCES
Philip preached in Caesarea (Acts 8:40; 21:8-9)
Peter preached to Cornelius, who was baptized (Acts 10)
Paul visited here in Acts 9:30 and was later imprisoned here (Acts 23:22 - 26:32)

PLAIN OF SHARON

As we depart Caesarea, we make our way north along the coastal plain known as the Plain of Sharon. This is a strip of land approximately 8-12 miles wide and 30 miles long located between the mountains of Carmel and the Mediterranean Sea . This strip runs from Joppa in the south to Mount Carmel in the north. It is fertile and beautiful like the "Lily of Sharon, the Rose of the Valley."

BIBLE REFERENCES
David's herds were pastured here (I Chronicles 27:25, 29)
Its splendor was spoken of by Isaiah (Isaiah 35:2; 65:10)

THE VIA MARIS

As we continue north and soon to be east, we travel a very famous ancient trade route known as the Via Maris, or the Way of the Sea. This route cuts through the Valley of Jezreel past Carmel and Megiddo and runs all the way into ancient Mesopotamia, a region known as the *fertile crescent.* Any world power controlling the Via Maris dominated the entire region.

MOUNT CARMEL

As we make our way northeast, we proceed to Mount Carmel. The name itself means *fruit garden.* Mount Carmel is a wedge-shaped mountain of limestone approximately 13 miles long. It divides the Plain of Acco to the north from the Plain of Sharon to the south. We'll ascend to the peak, which is 1810 feet above sea level. Here we'll have a fantastic view of the Valley of Jezreel. Mount Carmel is green year-round, and has been venerated since antiquity. The attraction of its garden-like beauty motivated the Egyptians and Canaanites to establish Mount Carmel as their center of worship for the pagan deity Baal in the time of Elijah and the prophets. Today, a Carmelite Monastery stands at the peak to commemorate Elijah's fiery confrontation with the false prophets of Baal.

BIBLE REFERENCES
Elijah's contest with the prophets of Baal was here (I Kings 18:19-40)
A 3½ year drought was ended here by Elijah's prayer (I Kings 18:41-45)

THE BROOK KISHON

As you stand on top of Mt. Carmel and look to the northeast, you will see the Brook Kishon just below. This small river flows past Carmel on its way to the Mediterranean. Brook Kishon is very shallow and is only about 25 miles in length. This is the site where Elijah slew the prophets of Baal (I Kings 18:40).

THE VALLEY OF JEZREEL

We now continue through the Valley of Jezreel, also known as the Valley of Esdraelon and the Valley of Armageddon. Jezreel is the largest and most fertile valley in Israel. Jezreel divides the mountains of Samaria (the heartland of Israel) in the south from those of Galilee to the north. Historically, this has been a major ancient battleground, with 21 Old Testament battles fought here. Because Israel is a land-bridge between Egypt to the south and Asia Minor/Europe to the north, this became the staging area and scene of battle between the Egyptians and their foes vying for power in the north. Hence, the Egyptians, Hittites, Israelites, Philistines, Assyrians, Babylonians, Medes-Persians, Greeks, Romans, Crusaders, Moslems, Turks, French and British have all fought here. In addition, God gave John a vision on the Isle of Patmos establishing this valley as the site of the end-time Battle of Armageddon (Rev. 16:16; Zechariah 12:10-11; Zechariah 14).

The Jezreel Valley has five mountain passes: Carmel, Nazareth, Moreh, Tabor and Gilboa. These passes served as entrances to the valley and each was protected by a fortress city. During the time of the dispersion of the Jewish people from the land of Israel and the subsequent occupation of Palestinian and Turkish Moslems, the Valley became a malaria-infested swamp. Photographs are available from the turn of the century that shows water buffalo lying in the swamp waters. Then in the early 1900's God's people began moving back into the region and purchased this land, at a very high price, from the Arabs. They began drying up the swamp through drainage and by the planting of Eucalyptus trees. Today this valley produces the highest volume of food per square foot in the world! We can now see the fulfillment of Biblical prophecy as God restores the land of Israel and it becomes "... *like the garden of Eden.*" (Ezekiel 36:35).

BIBLE REFERENCES
This area was allotted to the tribe of Issachar (Joshua 19: 17-23)
Deborah and Barak fought Sisera here (Judges 4-5)
This is the valley of Gideon's victory (Judges 7)
Here Elijah ran before Ahab's chariot (I Kings 18:46)

MEGIDDO

Our next stop is the fortress city of Megiddo. This was a royal city of the Canaanites and lies on the southern edge of the plain of Jezreel strategically located where the Via Maris enters the Valley of Jezreel (the Valley of Armageddon). This fortress city protected the greatest ancient trade route in the world. Under the shadow of this fortress passed the great armies of history and many of their most decisive battles were fought on the plain below. Thutmoses, Ramses, Shishak, Pharaoh Nacho, Sennacherib, Alexander the Great, Pompey, Titus, Saladin, Napoleon and General Allenby of the British all fought here! The very word *Armageddon* comes from Revelation 16:16 and means *the hill of Megiddo*.

Megiddo was occupied as early as 4000 B.C. Between 1925 and 1939, the University of Chicago did major excavations of the Biblical Tel that revealed 20 layers of major civilizations built one on top of the other from 4000 B.C. to 400 B.C. The excavations revealed a great deal about the time periods in the land and the cultures of the occupying peoples. A water system was found that dated back to 2800 B.C. and includes a water shaft 120 feet deep which connects with a spring located outside the walls of the city. Here we also find a sunken grain silo, stables for 450 horses built during Solomon's time, and a large, round, stone altar used by the Canaanites to sacrifice to their pagan gods. It is here at Megiddo we get our first glimpse of the stone watering and feeding troughs used in Israel to care for the animals; it is here we see the Bible's version of a manger, perhaps exactly like the one Mary lay baby Jesus in after His birth in Bethlehem.

BIBLE REFERENCES
Joshua killed the king and took the city (Joshua 12:7, 21)
The city was possessed by Manasseh (Joshua 17:11; I Chronicles 7:29)
Solomon fortified the city as one of his *chariot cities* (II Kings 9:15,19)
Ahaziah, king of Israel, was slain here by Jehu (II Kings 9:27)

NAZARETH

As we continue our journey, we make our way to the northern side of the Jezreel Valley and ascend the mountain of Nazareth, some 1230 feet above sea level, to the boyhood hometown of Jesus Christ. Nazareth is located on a brow of the mountain, midway between the Sea of Galilee and the Mediterranean Sea.

Nazareth is the place where Jesus lived with his mother, Mary, and his earthly dad, Joseph, a carpenter. Nazareth is the place where Jesus attended school in the local synagogue and worshipped with his family on the Sabbath (Luke 2:39, 51-52). It was here Mary first heard the Angel Gabriel's announcement of the birth of Jesus (Isaiah 7:14; Luke 1:26-38). It was here Christ entered the ministry at age 30. It was here, when after hearing Jesus proclaim the truth of the Scriptures, the people took Him to the brow of the city to throw Him to His death, and He walked through them undetected and made His way to Capernaum to begin His earthly ministry (Luke 4:16-31).

In Jesus' time, Nazareth was an obscure village (John 1:46). But today it is populated by a vast community of Moslems and Christian Arabs, as well as many Jewish people living in Upper Nazareth. The Nazareth Baptist Church and School are located here and have been responsible for starting many new churches in the region of Galilee.

BIBLE REFERENCES

Joseph and Mary left from Nazareth to go to Bethlehem where Jesus was to be born (Luke 2:1-7)

Joseph, Mary and Jesus returned to Nazareth from Egypt (Matthew 2:21-23)

Jesus left here when He was 30 to be baptized by John in the Jordan (Mark 1:9)

CANA

As we depart Nazareth, we make our way toward the Sea of Galilee and drive through a small village known as Kefar Cana, located only four miles to the east. Do not mistake this village as the Cana of Jesus' time. There is a Catholic Franciscan Church as well as a Greek Orthodox church located here; however, these sites are only traditional locations for Jesus' first miracle of turning the water into wine at the wedding feast (John 2:1-11).

BIBLE REFERENCES
Home of Nathanael (John 1:47; 21:2)
Jesus' first miracle (John 2:1-11)
Jesus healed the nobleman's son who was in Capernaum (John 4:46-54)

CONCLUSION OF DAY 1

As we continue to descend the Mountain of Nazareth, we get our very first glimpse of the Sea of Galilee, which lies 686 feet below sea level. It is breathtaking as we see the very waters Jesus calmed and later walked upon!

In a few minutes we will arrive at our hotel for dinner and a restful evening. Why not take a moment and silently praise the Lord Jesus Christ for the opportunity to experience all you have seen and heard this very day and ask Him to prepare your heart for tomorrow? Then, once all settled in, don't forget to read about tomorrow's sites and the related Scripture passages before retiring.

> **Special Note:** Many of the sights visited in Israel will be *traditional* sights. These are locations for which there is a valid basis according to tradition handed down from the 4th century. However, the Sea of Galilee and the cities surrounding it are authentic! Here Jesus calmed the storm, walked upon the water and at Jesus' command, Peter, too, walked upon the water. So today, as we make our way across the very waters upon which Jesus calmed and walked. Take a moment to praise Him for who He is, what He has done and is doing in your life, and that you have committed yourself to the God who is all-powerful!

NOTES

DAY 2

This morning we begin our day with a boat ride across the Sea of Galilee. However, before we get started, let's get familiar with:

TIBERIAS

Tiberias lies on the west side of the Sea of Galilee, about 10 miles south of Capernaum. This New Testament city was built by Herod Antipas in 26 A.D. and named in honor of Caesar Tiberius. Here Herod also constructed the finest Jewish synagogue ever built and as a result, the city became populated with Jews from all over Israel. Tiberias was the capital of Galilee under Agrippa the 1st and the Roman procurators and after the fall of Jerusalem in 70 A.D., many Jews moved from Jerusalem to Tiberias. The Bible never records Jesus being in Tiberias and some believe it is because Tiberias is built on a cemetery and Jesus would not defile himself by walking on this ground. This idea is an argument from silence because we know Jesus di many things that are not recorded in Scripture. The ancient city of Tiberias lies about four miles south of modern Tiberias at the base of the Bereniki Mountains. There are many hot springs located here; hence, today Tiberias is Israel's leading resort area and is the only city of any size located on the Sea of Galilee.

SEA OF GALILEE

The Sea of Galilee is 13-14 miles long by 7-8 miles wide, 130-157 feet deep, 686 feet below sea level, and 32 miles in circumference. The sea is fresh water and has several different names. It is known as *Chinnereth,* in the King James translation (Numbers 34:11; Joshua 12:3, 13:27), and *Gennesaret* in the New Testament. However, most Christians know it simply as the *Sea of Galilee* (Matthew 4:18, 15:29; Mark 1:16, 7:31; John 6:1). In Israel, it is best known as *Kinneret*, which means, "harp", because the sea is shaped like a harp. Several cities were located on the northwest shoreline including Tiberias, Magdala, Tabgha, Bethsaida, Capernaum and Chorazin. If you look toward the eastern shoreline you will see Gadara, one of the Decapolis cities (a league of ten cities east of the Sea of Galilee). Here Jesus healed the demoniac and the demons entered into the swine (Matthew 8:28-34). Continuing east is Kibbutz Ein Gev and immediately east is the Mount known as Hippos, so called because it resembles the back of a horse. Hippos also was a Decapolis city and both Greek and Roman ruins can be found there.

BIBLE REFERENCES

The tribe of Gad settled here (Deuteronomy 3:17; Joshua 13:27)
Jesus spoke to the multitudes from Peter's boat (Mark 3:7-12; Luke 5:1-3)
Jesus calmed the storm (Matthew 8:23-27)
Jesus walked upon the water (Matthew 14:22-33; John 6:16-21)
Jesus appeared here after the resurrection (Mark 14:28; John 21:1-23)

As we arrive on the northwestern shore of the Sea of Galilee we disembark our boat at the beautiful Kibbutz Nof Ginosar. Here you will see beautiful flowers and fruits such as oranges, lemons, Parmelo and especially bananas—yellow, pink and even red! Nof Ginosar is the largest of the Kibbutzim located around Galilee and is famous to-day because it was here, in 1987, where some of the kibbutz members discovered a fishing boat buried in the mud that dates back to Jesus' time! Today the boat is immersed in chemicals in a special pool to keep it from deteriorating and you can see an interesting video presentation about the discovery.

We now re-board our motor coach and make our way up the road a short distance to...

CAPERNAUM

Kefar Nahum (village of Nahum the prophet), better known to us as Capernaum, lies about 2-1/2 miles from where the Jordan River enters the Sea of Galilee and 10 miles from Tiberias. In Jesus' time, it was a custom station and the place of residence for the high Roman officer. Here the Romans built a synagogue for the Jews in the 1st century. Capernaum was Jesus' ministry base in Galilee. The Bible records that when Jesus left Nazareth, He came to Capernaum and it became the center of His ministry for the last 18-20 months of His life on Earth. Jesus performed more miracles here than anywhere, and, for this reason, placed a strong curse upon Capernaum as well as Chorazin and Bethsaida because of their failure to repent (Matthew 11:23-24). Capernaum had a population of about 10,000 people in Jesus' time. Here Zebedee lived with his family. James and John shared in a fishing company with Simon and Andrew of Bethsaida (but who also lived in Capernaum). Here Jesus healed Peter's mother-in-law (Matthew 8:14); called the disciples to be "fishers of men" (Matthew 4:13, 18-22); called Levi, the tax collector, who became Matthew and later wrote the Gospel according to Matthew'; and preached in the synagogue. We will stand on the very sites where these things occurred! So many things were witnessed here by the Jews and yet they did not believe! Today we see only the *ruins* of Capernaum, because it was destroyed by a great earthquake just as Jesus said...because the people would not repent!

BIBLE REFERENCES
Jesus made it "His own city" (Matthew 4:13-17)
Jesus called His disciples (Matthew 4:13, 18-22; 9:9-13)
Peter lived here (Matthew 8:5, 14)
Jesus taught in the synagogue (Luke 4:31-33)

Jesus healed the centurion's servant (Matthew 8:5-13)
Jesus raised Jairus' daughter from the dead (Matthew 9:18-26)
Jesus healed the woman who had an "issue of blood" (Matthew 9:20-22)
Jesus healed the nobleman's son (John 4:46-54)

MOUNT OF BEATITUDES

Our next stop is the top of a low hill overlooking the sea recognized as the traditional site of the Sermon on the Mount, the Mount of the Beatitudes. This site is located to the northwest of Capernaum. It is now the site of an Italian convent built by the Franciscan Sisters in 1937 with money donated by Benito Mussolini.

Many believe this to be the probable site where Jesus taught the beatitudes. However, this sermon seems to be a composite of the essentials of kingdom life taught by Jesus in His entire Galilean ministry. **Be sure to read Matthew 5-7 before visiting this site.** We'll have an incredible view of the lake and its surrounding area from this vantage point. If you'll look to the shoreline, you can see a natural amphitheater where Jesus could have sat and taught and be heard by the crowds.

TABGHA

Our next stop is the city of Tabgha (seven springs), one of the six cities located along the northwestern shoreline. Tabgha is located two miles from Capernaum and 7-1/2 miles north of Tiberias. Tradition establishes this as the site of the miracle of the multiplication of the loaves and fishes, because Luke 9:10 places that miracle near Bethsaida to the northeast. Today there stands a small chapel displaying a lovely mosaic that depicts this event dating back to the 4th century. Near the shore not far from the chapel are several springs of water from whence the name is derived.

BIBLE REFERENCES
The name Tabgha does not appear in Scripture.
Jesus fed the 5,000 and then the 4,000 near Bethsaida (Luke 9:10-17; John 6:1-14)

PETER'S CHAPEL

Not far from Tabgha we will visit a traditional site which marks Peter's encounter with the risen Christ as recorded in John 21:1-19. Today we see a small chapel with a statue near the water depicting Jesus forgiving Peter for his denial in Jerusalem. We do not know where this event took place but Scripture places it along the *"shore of the Sea of Galilee."*

BIBLE REFERENCES
Jesus told Peter to feed my lambs (John 21:1-19)

CHORAZIN

Just beyond the Mount of Beatitudes lies the basalt ruins of Chorazin. Chorazin was destroyed according to Jesus' curse upon it in the early 300's and has never been rebuilt.

BIBLE REFERENCES
Jesus cursed Chorazin (Matthew 11:21-22)

CAESAREA PHILIPPI

As we continue north from the Sea of Galilee we head toward Caesarea Philippi. Caesarea Philippi is located at the foot of Israel's highest mountain, Mt. Hermon. Here we will see Canaanite shrines to Baal-Hermon and Roman shrines to the Greek god Pan or Ban as pronounced by the Arabs (the Arabs cannot pronounce the letter "P", rather they sound a "P" like a "B," hence they call this city Banias). This is the mythological god who was half man and half animal. The Greeks named this city Paneas and it remained as such until Philip the tetrarch renamed it Caesarea Philippi to distinguish it from Caesarea on the coast in 4 B.C. after the death of Herod the Great. This city was the farthermost northern limit of Jesus' travels. We have no record of Him ever traveling farther north than this site. It was at this location Jesus asked the disciples, "Whom do men say that I am?" (Matthew 16:13ff). It was also at this place that Jesus began to explain to the disciples how He must go to Jerusalem and suffer and die (Matthew 17:1ff). In addition, this is the place where we will see the headwaters of the springs which make up the Jordan River. The river is comprised of three springs: the Banias, the Dan and the Hasbani. These three form the famed Jordan River which name comes from the Hebrew words Jor, which means *from*, and Dan. Hence, "from Dan."

BIBLE REFERENCES
The northern limit of Jesus' journeys to the north (Matthew 16:13; Mark 8:27)
Site of Peter's great confession (Matthew 16:13-20)

GOLAN HEIGHTS

We depart Caesarea Philippi to the east and make our way through the area known as the Golan Heights. The name means "circle" and lies to the east and northeast of the Sea of Galilee. We are told in Deuteronomy 4:41-43 and in Joshua 20:8 that Golan was a city and that it was assigned to the tribe of Manasseh. The city of Golan was the principal city in this heavily populated region. Later, the city was lost and the area itself became known as the Golan. At the end of W.W.I the area was given to the Syrians and they held this region until the Six Day War of June 1967. In the years prior to the Six Day War, the Syrians used this region as their outpost to overlook the entire Lower Galilee and oftentimes shelled the Israelis from their vantage point. Taking the Golan Heights was a very difficult task and cost the lives of 115 Israeli soldiers. This area is essential to Israel's security and, as such, must never be given back to the Syrians.

BIBLE REFERENCES
Moses assigned Golan to the tribe of Manasseh (Deuteronomy 4:41-43)
It was assigned to the sons of Gershom (Joshua 21:27; I Chronicles 6:71)

QUNEITRA

Today this city is deserted and lies in ruins; however, prior to 1967, it was occupied by more than 30,000 Syrian soldiers. Quneitra was the headquarters of the Syrian army in the Golan. The city lies 40 miles to the south of Damascus, Syria's capital.

As we depart Quneitra, we drive southwest toward the Sea of Galilee and just prior to re-entering Tiberias we view the 1st Century village of . . .

MAGDALA

Magdala is located four miles north of Tiberias on the road leading around the Sea of Galilee. You most likely have already guessed what famous lady came from this village. However, the village in Jesus' time was known as Migdal. The word Migdal means *guard tower*. The city had a fortress tower which protected the roads converging from the Valley of the Doves and the Plains of Gennesaret. Migdal was the home of Mary of Magdalene, or Mary of Migdal, from whom Jesus cast out seven demons and healed her (Luke 8:2). Jesus most likely visited here often as it would have been the first city He came to when He was on His way to Capernaum. This was also the place where Jesus came after He fed the 4,000, and it was here where the Pharisees and Sadducees sought a sign from Him. Migdal was a wealthy city in the 1st Century and a center of agriculture, fishing, shipbuilding and trade. Rabbinical tradition says the city was known for her sexual sins. The Jewish historian Josephus, governor of Galilee, fortified the city after the death of Jesus but the city fell to Titus between 67-70 A.D. At that time, 6,700 Jews were killed, another 6,000 were deported to Corinth to build the canal, and nearly 30,000 were auctioned off as slaves.

BIBLE REFERENCES
Home of Mary Magdalene (Luke 8:2; Mark 16:9)
Jesus came here after feeding the 4,000 (Matthew 15:39 - 16:4)

YARDENIT BAPTISMAL SITE

Our last stop of the day is the Baptismal site built by the nearby kibbutz. This lovely area allows believers the opportunity to be baptized in the waters of the Jordan. Although the area itself is in a cove of the Sea of Galilee, the waters of the Jordan River run through the sea from the north and continue their journey south to the Dead Sea. The area where Jesus was baptized by John as recorded in John 1:28-34, Bethabara, is located seven miles southeast of Jericho and is not accessible to tourists. The Yardenit site has dressing rooms for changing as well as baptismal robes and towels for a small fee.

CONCLUSION OF DAY 2

As we make our way back to our hotel, reflect on the places you have visited today, the emotions you have felt, and thank Him for the privilege of being in His land. Following dinner, you may want to take a stroll along the shores of the lake or visit the *"Galilee Experience"* located on the boardwalk area directly behind the Plaza Hotel. This unique, multimedia presentation of Jesus' ministry in Galilee is owned and operated by a Christian couple. Don't forget to check out their bookstore and gift shop as well. Before retiring for the evening, remember to look over tomorrow's Scripture passages and to pray for your family back home. *Lila Tov* ("Goodnight" in Hebrew)!

NOTES

DAY 3

This morning before going down to breakfast you should set your luggage outside your door for the porters to collect. Following breakfast we will depart Tiberias driving south and then east. Our first stop of the day will be:

EIN HAROD (GIDEON'S SPRING)

The name Harod means *error or trembling*. The name most probably came from the fact that the Midianites became terrified as God routed them with a handful of soldiers led by Gideon. This was the place where the Lord led Gideon and his men, and it was here where He separated them, sending all but 300 home and keeping the small number to do battle as recorded in Judges 7. The spring is located north of Mt. Gilboa and today the water runs from under the mountain. It was here where Saul encamped the night before his death in the Philistine battle. Today, this site is one of Israel's national parks. As we drive away from Ein Harod, Mt. Gilboa is on our right.

BIBLE REFERENCES
Gideon fought against the Midianites (Judges 7)
Saul encamped here (I Samuel 29:1)

MOUNT GILBOA

The name Gilboa means *bubbling fountain.* This mountain is 10 miles long and rises 1696 feet above sea level. Here King Saul and his three sons, Jonathan, Abinadad and Malki-Shua died - the sons at the hands of the Philistines and Saul by his own hand (I Samuel 31:1-6). David cursed Gilboa as recorded in II Samuel 1:17-27 as he lamented the deaths of Saul and especially Jonathan, his dear friend.

BIBLE REFERENCES
Site of Saul and sons' deaths (I Samuel 31:1-6)
David curses Gilboa (II Samuel 1:17-27)

BEIT ALPHA

Kibbutz Beit Alpha is the location of the best preserved mosaic of an ancient synagogue in Israel. Beit Alpha is located at the foot of Mt. Gilboa in the Valley of Jezreel. During the swamp-draining efforts of the early settlers in 1928, ruins of a 6th Century synagogue with an elaborate mosaic floor were discovered. The mosaic floor is divided into three panels: (1) Abraham's would-be sacrifice of Isaac; (2) a zodiac wheel; (3) a group of religious ornaments, such as the ark of the law and the candelabra. Nearby, the kibbutz is a national park with warm springs and pools.

BETH SHEAN

Beth Shean or Beth Shan means *house of security.* This city protected the entrance to the Valley of Jezreel from the Jordan Valley. Beth Shean was inhabited as early as 3000 B.C. Excavations have revealed 18 levels of occupation with six pagan temples. The city was inherited by the tribe of Manasseh but they could never subdue the Canaanites at Beth Shean (Judges 1:27). The Old Testament city walls of Beth Shean was the location where the Philistines hung the bodies of Saul and his sons after their deaths and it was from here the men of Jabesh-Gilead took down their bodies for burial. The New Testament city of Beth Shean, built by the Romans, was one of the cities of the Decapolis, or ten cities. It was the only one of the ten west of the Jordan River, and, as such, became a very important city. During the time of Jesus, the city became known as Scythopolis, or the "city of the skit". The city was destroyed by an earthquake in the 8th century and was not rebuilt until 1949, when the Israelis began to do so. Today, Beth Shean is one of the largest archaeological excavation projects underway in Israel. Recent excavations have revealed a beautiful city with magnificent temples, streets, theaters and Israel's only amphitheater. It was this theater where the Romans watched as the Jews and Christians alike fought wild animals.

BIBLE REFERENCES
Beth Shan was a part of Manasseh's inheritance (Judges 1:27)
Saul and his sons' bodies hung here (I Samuel 31:8-13)

THE JORDAN VALLEY
We depart Beth Shean driving south through the Jordan River Valley. The Jordan River Valley is part of the Great Syro-African Rift formed by volcanic activity. It extends some 5500 miles from Turkey to Mozambique, Africa. The lowest point in this rift is the Dead Sea at 1300 feet below sea level. The Jordan River will be our constant companion for our entire journey as it winds its way on our left side from Dan in the north to the Dead Sea in the south. The Jordan River is the

boundary line today between Israel and her neighbor to the east, Jordan. The Jordan River is the only river in the world which runs its entire course below sea level.

The Jordan River Valley is a very important area today as well as in the past. From May 1948 until June 1967 the Israeli border to the east was the Old City of Jerusalem. However, in June 1967, the Israelis pushed the Jordanians eastward out of the Old City of Jerusalem and across the Jordan River establishing the river as the border. Prior to 1967, it was from this area the PLO would attempt to infiltrate Israel and commit acts of sabotage. After 1967, the valley was the scene of nightly military and terrorist activity until 1973 when things quieted down. What was once barren and deserted land has now become rich in agriculture on both sides of the river. A number of kibbutzim are now established along the valley and bring forth an abundant amount of fresh vegetables, grapes, and dates, as well as fresh flowers, etc. The mighty rushing Jordan River is not so mighty these days due to the fact that both the Israelis and the Jordanians are diverting water from it for irrigation purposes. The Jordan Valley of the Old Testament was also a lush and rich agricultural area.

BIBLE REFERENCES
Lot chose the plains of the Jordan (Genesis 13:10-11)
Israel miraculously crossed it and gathered stones from the bottom (Joshua 3:13-17; 4:1-9, 20-24)
John baptized many here (Matthew 3:6)
Jesus was baptized here (Matthew 3; Mark 1:4-11)
Jesus called His first disciples here (John 1:25-51)

MOUNT OF TEMPTATION

Just west of Jericho is the traditional site of the Mount of Temptation, known as Quarantana, where Jesus went to be alone with the Father and after which He was tested. There is a Greek monastery on the top of the mountain.

BIBLE REFERENCES
Jesus fasted and was tempted by Satan (Luke 4:1-13)

ELISHA'S WELL

Just across the street from the Tel of Jericho is the well which Elisha healed by throwing salt into it. The water still flows today and serves to irrigate the area.

BIBLE REFERENCES
Elisha healed its waters (II Kings 2:19-22)

BETHLEHEM

As we continue from Jericho up to Jerusalem, we enter Jerusalem briefly, then make our way south about six miles to the village of Bethlehem. As we journey this road, we are following the steps of Jacob and his family as they traveled from Bethel to Bethlehem. It was while they were on this journey that, at Bethlehem, Rachel died giving birth to Benjamin and was buried "on the way" (Genesis 35:16-20). Rachel's

Tomb will be seen on our right as we enter Bethlehem. The name "Bethlehem" means *house of bread*, coming from the two Hebrew words: "Bet" (*house of*) and "lehem" (*bread*). The village of Bethlehem has been and is a very significant location. It was here that Naomi and her daughter-in-law, Ruth, came at the beginning of the barley harvest and where Ruth later met and married Boaz and became the grand-mother of King David (Ruth 1ff, Samuel 17:12). Bethlehem was the home of Jesse and his son David who was to be the King of Israel (I Samuel 16:1-17). It was to this city that Joseph came with Mary, and Jesus was born (Matthew 2:1-6). It was here that the shepherds heard the angels proclaim the birth of the Messiah (Luke 2:8-20). And, it was here that all male children two years and under were ordered massa-cred by King Herod (Matthew 2:16).

The most important site we will visit in Bethlehem is the Church of the Nativity located in the heart of the village in Manger Square. As far as we know, this is the oldest Christian church in the world built by Queen Helena, the mother of the Roman Emperor Constantine, in 325 A.D. The church was constructed over the cave where scholars believe Christ was born. The building we will visit before descending to the cave below was enlarged and redesigned during the reign of Justinian in 527-565 A.D. It was later altered by the Crusaders during the occupation from 1099-1187. Today the church is jointly controlled by the Armenians, Greek Orthodox, and Roman Catholic churches. Unfortunately, this church detracts from the spirit of the location of Christ's birth as it is covered with "religious items" and stands today as a testimony of what man's religion can do. We will descend to the cave below the church known as The Grotto and here view the site of Christ's birth. The cave itself has been decorated on the inside and as a result one hardly recognizes it as a cave. However, we must not let the surroundings detract us lest we forget THE EVENT!

Not far from Manger Square, we can see the Shepherd's Field where even today, as 2,000 years ago, shepherds still tend their flocks.

BIBLE REFERENCES

The story of Ruth and Boaz takes place here (see the Book of Ruth)
Site of David's anointing as king (I Samuel 16:1-14, 17:12)
David was a shepherd boy here (I Samuel 17:15, 34-37)
David went from here to Saul's army to slay Goliath (I Samuel 17:12-58)
Micah foretold Christ's birth (Micah 5:2; Matthew 2:4-6)
Matthew and Luke recount Jesus' birth (Matthew 1:18-25; Luke 2:1-7)

_____

_____

_____

_____

_____

_____

_____

_____

_____

_____

_____

_____

Bethlehem is such a significant site and is mentioned so many times in Scripture, it is impossible to record all the events. Therefore only a very few are listed.

As we depart Bethlehem, we will be stopping at one of the many gift stores located in the village for your convenience.

CONCLUSION OF DAY 3

Our next stop will be our hotel in Jerusalem. As this very exciting day draws to a close, pause and thank our precious Lord once again for the privilege of being in this place, to walk where He walked, to see with your own eyes the sites you have read about in His Word, and to share in the sweet fellowship of His people.

Remember to take time this evening to prepare yourself for tomorrow. Please read your program and the related Scriptures, and, before you go to sleep, pray for your loved ones back home! Lila Tov!

NOTES

DAY 4

"I rejoiced with those who said to me, 'Let us go to the house of the Lord.' Our feet are standing in your gates, O Jerusalem. Jerusalem is built like a city that is closely compacted together. That is where the tribes go up, the tribes of the Lord, to praise the name of the Lord according to the statute given to Israel. There the thrones for judgment stand, the thrones of the house of David. Pray for the peace of Jerusalem: 'May those who love you be secure. May there be peace within your walls and security within your citadels.'" Ps. 122:1-7.

"As the mountains surround Jerusalem, so the Lord surrounds his people both now and forevermore." Ps. 125:1-2.

"Walk about Zion, go around her, count her towers, consider well her ramparts, view her citadels, that you may tell them to the next generation. For this God is our God for ever and ever; he will be our GUIDE even to the end." Ps. 48:12-14.

JERUSALEM

Welcome to the most important City in the world! Jerusalem has been, is, and always will be at the very heart of the issues of the world in which we live. It is God's city! This city, whose name means *"peace,"* has had more wars fought over her than any city in history. Jerusalem has been known through the centuries as Jebus, Salem, City of Peace, Zion, City of David, Aelia Capitolina, the Holy City and the

Golden City. Jerusalem is located in the tops of the Judean Mountain range about 3000 feet above sea level (2740 feet to be precise), 38 miles from the Mediterranean Sea and 14 miles from the Dead Sea as the crow flies.

In about 1000 B.C., David made Jerusalem the capital of Israel when he moved from Hebron and brought the Ark of the Covenant to dwell here (2 Samuel 5:6-16; 6:1-2). Solomon, his son, made the city beautiful by building palaces, strengthening her walls, and building The Temple, the dwelling place of God! After the death of Solomon the twelve tribes of Israel were divided (I Kings 12) into the Northern and Southern Kingdoms with ten tribes in the north and two in the south. Israel and Judea had many kings, some good, but most bad!

In 722 B.C., the Northern Kingdom was attacked by the Assyrians under Sennacherib and the people were required to pay heavy tribute (2 Kings 18:3-16) to Assyria. Many were led captive to the north and lost to history, but not to God. These became known as the LOST TRIBES of ISRAEL.

In 609 B.C., Pharaoh Necho of Egypt captured Jerusalem for the Egyptians. However, this was short-lived, for in the spring of 605 B.C., Nebuchadnezzar of Babylon laid siege to the city and carried away many captives until finally, in 586 B.C., the city fell. The Jewish people remained in captivity in Babylon until their 70 years of prophesied captivity came to an end, and they were allowed to return to the land under the Medo-Persian King Cyrus in the spring of 536 B.C. The city walls were repaired under the leadership of Nehemiah and the Temple and religious life repaired under the leadership of Ezra the scribe, and Zerubbabel (Ezra 1).

Alexander the Great captured Jerusalem in 332 B.C., and in 320 B.C., one of Alexander's four generals, Ptolemy Soter, took it. In 302 B.C., Jerusalem was annexed to Egypt and later came under the control of the Greek, Antiochus Epiphanies of Macedonia. When this pagan ordered a pig slain on the alter of the Temple, the Jewish people had had enough, and the rebellion of the Maccabees broke out, led by Judas Maccabees. The revolt led to the expulsion of the Greeks. The Jews were one again in control of the land and their lives and ruled by Hasmonean kings from 167 B.C. to about 63 B.C. when they were invaded by Rome. The Romans appointed Herod the Great to rule over the Jews in 37 B.C., and he set about building great cities and harbors and beautifying the Temple in Jerusalem even more than Solomon.

Herod the Great died in about 4 B.C., thus the Jerusalem Jesus knew was the one beautified by Herod. The Jewish people lost their country, their land, their cities, and even their religious freedom because they failed to be what God intended them to be. Because of Israel's rebellion against God, they were dominated by foreign powers until 66 A.D., when they revolted against Rome. Titus, the grandson of the Roman Emperor Vespasian, was sent to put down the revolt. The prophecy of Jesus spoken on the Mount of Olives and recorded in Matthew 24 became a reality. Jerusalem was destroyed, the Temple leveled, and the city burned. Thousands of Jews lost their lives, and finally in. 73 A.D, Masada, the last stronghold, fell. Rome had won, and the Jewish people were scattered from the land God had given to them into all the world, in the event known as the Great Diaspora or scattering. A small group of Jews remained in the land until 135 A.D. when Bar Kokhba led another revolt, and this time, Hadrian, the Roman Emperor, finished what Titus had begun. He literally ordered his soldiers to plow asunder the Temple Mount area, thus fulfilling to the letter Jesus' prophecy: *"not one stone here will be left upon another; every one will be thrown down."* (Matthew 24:2).

Further, Hadrian rebuilt the city, renamed it Aelia Capitolina, and forbid that anyone call it Jerusalem under penalty of death. He built pagan temples on sacred sites and Jews were banned from the city. Hadrian also changed the name of Israel from Judea to Syria Palestina or Syria of the Philistines, hence, the name, Palestine (Isaiah 14:29, 31).

And so it remained until the Roman emperor, Constantine, in 332 A.D., converted to Christianity. He then ordered his mother, Queen Helena, to begin to build churches on the sacred sites, the oldest being the Church of the Nativity in Bethlehem in 325 A.D. Constantine's conversion brought about a split in the Roman Empire, as prophesied in Daniel 2; and the eastern half of the Roman Empire became known as the Byzantium Empire with its capital at Constantinople, modern-day Istanbul. The Byzantines remained in control of Israel until the Persians took Jerusalem on May 20, 614 A.D., and killed more than 33,000 Jews and Christians.

Then, in 637 A.D., a new religion, Islam, founded by Mohammed (born in 570), dominated Israel and began to spread throughout the Middle East. Finally in 1009, a Muslim leader, Fatimid Caliph Hakim, ordered the destruction of the Church of the Holy Sepulcher, thus sparking the Crusades from Europe which took place from 1099-1187.

The Mamelukes from Egypt came into power until 1517, when the Ottoman Turkish Empire dominated this part of the world.

Israel, called Palestine, remained under the Turks' control until the end of WWI, when it was liberated under General Allenby and his British forces, and entered the time known as the British Mandate, 1917 to 1948.

Then, on May 14, 1948, Israel became an independent state and modern-day Israel was re-born; however, Jerusalem was a divided city! The Old City of Jerusalem, that is, the part enclosed by the city walls, remained under the control of the Arab Palestinians until the Six Day War of June 1967, when it, along with the land east to the Jordan River, the Golan Heights in the north, and the Sinai in the south, was taken by the Israelis. With the Old City regained, Jerusalem became a united city, under Jewish control for the first time in over 1900 years, and once again the Jewish people had access to their sacred sites. The Old City walls that stand today have been destroyed and rebuilt at least five times, the last being by Suleiman the Magnificent in 1542. There are eight gates and 34 towers and the walls are 2½ miles in length and average 40 feet in height.

It is often said Jerusalem is home to the three great religions of the world, Judaism, Islam and Christianity. However, we must never say this, for Jerusalem is home to two of the world's religions and "THE WAY!" Christianity must never be placed on the level of man's religions, but stands alone as Jesus Christ reaching down to sinful man and reconciling man to Himself through the shedding of His innocent blood.

BIBLE REFERENCES
Jerusalem is mentioned more than 800 times in the Bible.

MOUNT SCOPUS

This morning as you look over the city of Jerusalem you will be standing on Mount Scopus, meaning "to look over," looking to the south. Mt. Scopus is connected to the Mount of Olives on the northern end and has always been a strategic location. This is the area where the Roman legions under Titus camped in 70 A.D., the Crusaders in 1099, the British in 1917, and the Arabs in 1948 and 1967. We will drive along the top of Scopus this morning headed south to the Mount of Olives. Along the way we will pass the British War Cemetery, the Hebrew University, the Truman Research Center and the Augusta Victoria Hospital.

MOUNT OF OLIVES

Our first stop today will be atop the Mount of Olives. This limestone ridge is located between Bethany to the east and Jerusalem to the west. It rises 240 feet above the Temple Mount area and is separated from it by the Kidron Valley, also known as the Valley of Jehoshaphat. As we stand looking west from the top of the mount, we will see several sites that must be mentioned before we begin our descent to the Garden of Gethsemane below.

Jewish Cemetery, located just below, is the largest and oldest Jewish cemetery in the world dating back to biblical times. The Jews believe the final judgment and resurrection will take place here.

61

Palm Sunday Path is to the left and is the traditional road most believe Jesus traveled as He made His Triumphal entry into Jerusalem (Luke 19:28ff). It descends from the Mount of Olives, goes across the Kidron Valley, and up through the Eastern Gate into the Temple area.

Dominus Flevit Chapel, Latin for "our Lord cries or weeps," is a Franciscan church and is not very old. This small chapel is the traditional site where Jesus stopped, looked over the city of Jerusalem and wept (Matthew 23:37-39; Luke 19:41-44).

Russian Orthodox Church of Mary Magdalene is a little farther down and to the north of Dominus Flevit. It can be easily recognized by its seven onion-shaped spires. It was built in 1888 by Alexander the III and is maintained today by the White Russian nuns.

The Church of All Nations is located in the Garden of Gethsemane and is the largest building in the area. This church was built in 1924 on the site of a Crusader church, and inside is the traditional Rock of Agony where Jesus was to have prayed.

BIBLE REFERENCES
Jesus taught the Mount of Olives discourse (Matthew 24)
David fled over the Mount of Olives from Absalom (II Samuel 15:30; 16:14)
Scene of the Triumphal entry (Luke 19:28-44)
The fig tree was cursed (Matthew 21:17-22)
Place of the ascension of Jesus (Acts 1:4-12)
Mount will be split at Second Coming of Christ (Zechariah 14:4)

GARDEN OF GETHSEMANE
The Garden of Gethsemane, which means *garden of the wine press*, is located at the base of the Mount of Olives and is maintained by the Franciscans. This beautiful garden contains eight ancient olive trees,

claimed by botanists to be over 3,000 years old. However, the historian, Josephus, records that Titus cut down all the trees in the environs of Jerusalem in 70 A.D. Whether or not these trees were spared or they grew later from their deep roots, we do not know. We do know, however, it was to this area Jesus came often and prayed. Especially on the last night of His life on earth. We will depart the traditional garden area and step across the narrow Palm Sunday path and there enter a private garden where we will have a wonderful time of praise and prayer.

BIBLE REFERENCES

Gethsemane was a garden across the Kidron. John 18:1
It was across from the Golden Gate. Luke 22:39
Here Jesus took upon himself the sins of mankind. Matthew 26:36-56; Luke 22:39-53
Site of betrayal of Jesus and His arrest. Matthew 26:47-56; John 18:1-13

_____

_____

_____

_____

KIDRON VALLEY

The Kidron Valley, also known as the Valley of Jehoshaphat, is a Wadi about three miles north to south, lying between Jerusalem and the Mount of Olives. The valley is the site of four tombs: Absalom's Pillar, Tomb of Jehoshaphat, Grotto of St. James and Tomb of Zechariah.

BIBLE REFERENCES

Burying Israelites in the valley was a custom (II Kings 23:6)
David fled over the Kidron Valley from Absalom (II Samuel 15:13-23)
Jesus crossed the Kidron Valley (John 18:1)

_____

_____

_____

LION'S GATE

As we depart the Garden of Gethsemane, our next stop will be the Old City of Jerusalem. We enter the Old City through the Lion's Gate, also known as St. Stephen's Gate. This gate, one of eight, is on the east side of the city and was built with reliefs of lions on it, due to a dream of the Sultan Suleiman, hence, the name. It is also called St. Stephen's Gate because tradition has it that Stephen was stoned near here.

BIBLE REFERENCES
Stephen was martyred near here (Acts 7:54-60)

CHURCH OF ST. ANNE

As we proceed west, we visit the Church of St. Anne. This Crusader church was built in 1100 A.D. on the site of a Byzantine church which had, in turn, been built over the cave believed to have been the home of Joachim and Anne, parents of Mary, mother of Jesus. Our visit will be to observe perhaps the finest example of Crusader construction in Israel as well as to sing and hear the beautiful acoustics of the church.

POOL OF BETHESDA

Located adjacent to St. Anne's Church is the pool of Bethesda, which means *house of mercy*. This ancient pool, which is only partially excavated, is about 60 feet below the present ground level. The pool, according to Scripture, had five porticos or porches.

Jesus healed a lame man (John 5:1-16)

_____

_____

_____

_____

As we exit the St. Anne area we turn right and proceed west along a portion of the Via Dolorosa, the Way of the Cross. We look up the way and see the Ecco Homo Arch, "behold the man" in Latin, built over the Via Dolorosa. This arch was built by Hadrian in the 2nd century, and is a section of a triple gateway leading to the rebuilt city of Aelia Capitolina. The arch also points us to our next stop…

ANTONIA FORTRESS

Today this site is called the Sisters of Zion Convent or the Ecco Homo Convent. This is so because the site is built over the "pavement" area of the Antonia Fortress, site of Pilate's Courtyard where Jesus was condemned to the cross. Upon the stones, which are today about 30 feet below street level, we can see the area called the Lithostrotos, paved squares where the Romans marked the stones in order to play their games of fun. One such game is known as _Basilicus_. This game was the one most likely played with Jesus as the Basil or King (Matthew 27:27-30). This area was adjacent to the Temple area to the north. Here we will have a special time of prayer as we contemplate His suffering and death for our sin.

BIBLE REFERENCES
Here was location of tower of Hananeel in Nehemiah's day (Nehemiah 3:1; 12:39)
Jesus before Pilate (Matthew 27:2, 11-31)

_____

_____

_____

MOUNT ZION

We ascend Mt. Zion (fortress) to visit the traditional site of the Upper Room and the Tomb of King David. Here we say "traditional" because the Mt. Zion of today and the Mt. Zion of David's time are two different locations. The Zion of David's time was north of the area of the Pool of Siloam, and the Gihon Spring occupied by David was just south of Mt. Moriah (Temple Mount). We know this because of the 48th Psalm. In this Psalm, David says Zion is to the north. In Jesus' time, Mt. Zion, then inside the Old City Walls but now outside the walls, was relocated to the southwest part of the city. In addition, Mt. Zion is another name for Jerusalem.

UPPER ROOM

We visit the traditional site of the First Supper. This upper room serves only to allow us an opportunity to remember the last meal Christ shared with His followers. The building housing the Upper Room dates only to 1335 and was used as a Moslem Mosque until 1967.

BIBLE REFERENCES
Traditional site of the Last Supper (Matthew 26:17-30; John 13:1-30)
Location of the giving of the Holy Spirit on Pentecost (Acts 2:1-42)

HOUSE OF CAIAPHAS

We end our day at the Palace of the High Priest Caiaphas. Today this house is outside the Old City. However, in Jesus' time it was inside the Old City walls and just southwest of the Temple complex. This site is also called Saint Peter's In Gallicantu, or the place of the cock crow, because it is the site where Peter denied Jesus three times before the rooster crowed. The church standing today was built in 1931 over the site where the palace originally stood. In the basement we will visit an area where Jesus may have been held during the night before His appearance before Pilate. In addition, we will see the courtyard area where Peter most probably warmed himself by the fire and was confronted as being one of Jesus' followers.

BIBLE REFERENCES
This was the scene of the first trial (Matthew 26:57-63)
Here Peter denied the Lord three times (John 18:15-18, 25-27)

CONCLUSION OF DAY 4

As our day draws to a close and we make our way back to our hotel, review all you have seen, heard and felt today. What a joy it is to personally know Jesus Christ as Savior and Lord. Just think, *God made him who had no sin to be sin for us, so that in him we might become the righteousness of God* (2 Corinthians 5:21). Wow, what a Friend we have in Jesus!

NOTES

DAY 5

Today we will continue our time in Jerusalem by visiting sites in both the Old and New city. Our morning begins early.

TEMPLE MOUNT

We now ascend the walk up to Temple Mount. This area of roughly 27 acres is the top of Mount Moriah. This is the place where, as recorded in Gen. 22, God directed Abraham to bring his only son Isaac and prepare to offer him as a sacrifice. This is the place where, as recorded in 2 Samuel 24, God stops the plague and David buys the threshing floor from Araunah the Jebusite. This is the site where Solomon builds the Temple to God, which was first destroyed by the Babylonians in 586 B.C. and where the second Temple of Jesus' time was re-built during the days of Zerubbabel, Nehemiah, and Ezra and later enlarged and beautified by Herod the Great. Today, the Temple area is under the control of the Moslems in an effort to keep peace. The Temple is gone and in its place is the Moslem Shrine known as the Dome of The Rock. This shrine was built between 687-691 A.D. and is decorated with blue, green, yellow and white Persian tiles. The dome rises some 108 feet above the ground and is covered with an aluminum bronze alloy from Italy. This shrine was used as a church by the Crusaders from 1099-1187. The Dome of the Rock is used for individual prayers, while on the southern end of the area is the lead-domed El Aksa Mosque where the Moslems gather for group prayers. This is the site where King Abdullah of Jordan was assassinated in 1951, thereby allowing for his grandson, King Hussein, to become the ruler of Jordan. El Aksa means *distant place* with reference to its being far removed from Mecca.

WAILING WALL

The Wailing or Western Wall is a portion of the retaining wall Herod built around the western side of the Temple Mount and is the holiest shrine in the Jewish world today. The wall today is holy to the Jews because this portion is all that was left of the Temple compound from 70 A.D. when Titus of Rome destroyed the Temple and the City of Jerusalem. The portion of the wall that is today exposed in 60 yards in length and about 60 feet high. Each Friday evening, as the Sabbath begins, one can see great crowds of Jews gathering at the wall to pray. In addition, almost any time of the day or night one can see people at the wall praying. You may want to write a prayer on a small piece of paper to put into a crack between the stones of the wall before we visit this site and pray there.

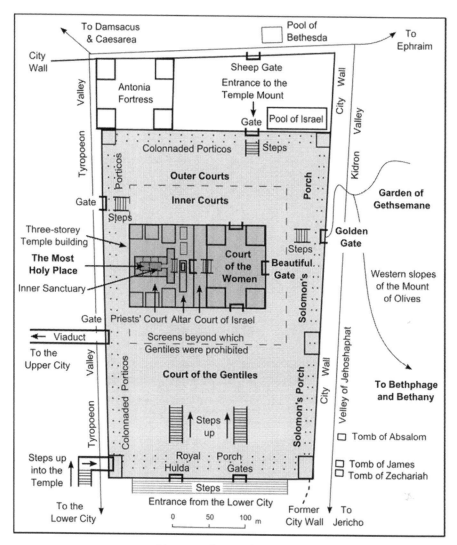

Diagram of Herod's Temple

The following labels appear on the diagram:

To Damsacus & Caesarea

Pool of Bethesda

To Ephraim

City Wall

Valley

Antonia Fortress

Sheep Gate
Entrance to the Temple Mount

City Wall

Gate | Pool of Israel

Valley

Tyropoeon Valley

Porticos

Colonnaded Porticos | Steps

Kidron Valley

Outer Courts

Porch

Garden of Gethsemane

Gate | Inner Courts

Steps

Three-storey Temple building

Steps

Golden Gate

The Most Holy Place

Court of the Women

Steps

Inner Sanctuary

Beautiful Gate

Western slopes of the Mount of Olives

Gate | Priests' Court Altar Court of Israel

Solomon's

Viaduct

Screens beyond which Gentiles were prohibited

To the Upper City

Valley

Colonnaded Porticos

Court of the Gentiles

Solomon's Porch

City Wall

Velley of Jehoshaphat

To Bethphage and Bethany

Tyropoeon

Steps up

☐ Tomb of Absalom

Steps up into the Temple

Royal Porch
Hulda Gates

☐ Tomb of James
☐ Tomb of Zechariah

To the Lower City

Steps
Entrance from the Lower City

Former City Wall

To Jericho

0   50   100 m

SOUTHERN STEPS

An expansive Herodian staircase that led to the triple-arched entrance and double-arched exit known as the Hulda Gates was discovered soon after the Israeli government gained control of the Temple Mount in 1967. The staircase, 215 feet wide containing 30 steps that alternate between wide and narrow to discourage running, was where Jesus ascended each time He entered the Temple, pausing first to purify Himself in one of the many "ritual baths." Since it was the custom for rabbi to teach their followers on the steps leading from the double-arched gate, Jesus most likely paused here often to teach the Twelve Disciples. It is believed that "A Psalm of Ascents" (a song of pilgrims ascending to Jerusalem comprised of Psalms 124-130) was sung as the Jews ascended to Jerusalem every year for the their feasts.

CITY OF DAVID

Older than the city that lies within Jerusalem's walls, the Biblical City of David is where King David once lived and ruled. Three thousand years ago, King David conquered Jerusalem from the Jebusites and decided to build the city as the capital of Israel. For more than 1,000 years the City of David housed the kings, prophets and people that fill the pages of the Bible. After centuries of neglect, the City of David was buried under the sands of time and forgotten. In recent years, archaeological excavations have uncovered stunning evidence of both First and Second Temple Period Jerusalem.

THE MODEL CITY

On the west side of Jerusalem near the Knesset at the Israel Museum is a model of the city of Jerusalem of Herod's time, 66 A.D. It took seven years to finish his model and it is on a scale of 1 to 50 (¼ inch = 1 foot). The model cost about one million dollars and was constructed by a father in memory of his son who was killed in the war of 1967. This model visually helps the visitor to understand the location of key places such as Temple Mount, Calvary, etc., in relationship to the rest of the city as well as the line of the city walls. You may take photos of the model; however, video cameras are not allowed.

THE SHRINE OF THE BOOK MUSEUM

Located across the street from the Knesset is the famous Israel Museum which houses the Shrine of the Book. This building is easily recognized by the onion-shaped top that was constructed to resemble the top of the stone jar in which the Dead Sea Scrolls were found.

As we make our way across Jerusalem, we proceed back to the east side of the Old City where we enter through the Zion Gate. You will want to look closely at this gate and, as you do, you will see the numerous bullet holes in the stone from the Six Day War of June 1967. Once the Israeli soldiers broke through this gate they made their way to the Wailing Wall and took control of the Old City.

THE MONASTERY OF THE CROSS

As we make our way in West Jerusalem, we will pass the Monastery of the Cross, located in the Valley of the Cross. This monastery was built in the 11th century on the traditional site where the tree came from upon which Christ was crucified. I stress the tradition of this since it is not possible to know this for certain. Today the Greek Orthodox Church maintains the grounds. In addition, they claim the cypress trees in the courtyard are shoots from the original trees planted by Lot when he came here after the destruction of Sodom.

THE KNESSET

We will also view the Knesset, which is Israel's Parliament Building. This building was built on the "acropolis" of Jerusalem at a cost of 7 million dollars. In front of the building stands a large 16-foot high bronze Menorah donated to Israel by Britain. The Israeli Parliament consists of 120 elected members.

CONCLUSION OF DAY 5

We now return to our hotel for dinner and overnight. Just when you thought it couldn't get any better, it does! Remember to thank the Lord for the privilege of being in His land tonight before you retire and ask Him to prepare your heart for all He has for us tomorrow!

NOTES

DAY 6

This morning we depart Jerusalem for a full-day adventure to the Dead Sea area. We will take the road out of the city eastward toward Jericho and the Jordan River Valley descending from 3000 feet above sea level to 1200 feet below sea level. This 4200-foot change in altitude means it should be considerably warmer in the valley than in Jerusalem. Once we arrive in the valley, we will turn south and drive along the shores of the Dead Sea, the lowest point on earth. Our first stop today will be:

JUDEAN WILDERNESS

The Judean Wilderness lies east of Jerusalem and is bordered by the Mountains of Juda to the west and the Dead Sea to the east. It is only 580 square miles but has many unique features, including numerous valleys and many deep ravines (up to 1,200 feet). Because of its lack of water and good routes, the Judean wilderness has been (mostly) uninhabited throughout history. Consequently, it as an ideal place for those seeking refuge from enemies or retreat from the world. When on the run from King Saul, David hid in various places in the Judean wilderness (the Wilderness of Ziph, Maon, and Ein Gedi are part of the Judean Wilderness). John the Baptist preached here and it seems likely that this was the wilderness where Jesus was tempted. Herod the Great built two fortresses (Herodium and Masada) in this area for protection should his people ever revolt against him.

QUMRAN

The ancient remains of Qumran, an Essene community, was the site of the discovery of the Dead Sea Scrolls in the spring of 1947. It was the most significant archaeological find of the 20th Century! Prior to this discovery, the most recent copy of the Scriptures was the 6th Century A.D. This find now gave us copies that date from 300 B.C. to 70 A.D. and exactly match, letter-for-letter, word-for-word, with the 6th Century copies. Today many of the scrolls are housed in the Israel Museum in Jerusalem.

MASADA

Masada, the Judean fortress fortified by Herod is situated on the top of an isolated rock plateau overlooking the Judean desert panorama to the west and the Dead Sea to the east. Masada was fortified between 31 and 37 A.D. as a refuge for Herod in the event of a revolt. The thrilling story of the site reveals the courage of the Jewish defenders of Masada and their battle against the conquering Romans. In 73 A.D. Masada, which was the last stronghold held by the Jewish Zealots, was captured by the Romans.

EIN-GEDI

Ein Gedi is located on the western shore of the Dead Sea and is the largest desert oasis in Israel. The abundant springs and year-round temperature climate provided the perfect conditions for agriculture in ancient times. Solomon compared his lover to "a cluster of henna blossoms from the vineyards of Ein Gedi," an indication of the beauty and fertility of the site.

Around 1000 B.C., Ein Gedi served as one of the main places of refuge for David as he fled from Saul. David "dwelt in the strongholds at Ein Gedi." Ein Gedi means literally "the spring of the kid (goat)." Evidence exists that young ibex have always lived near the springs of Ein Gedi. One time when David was fleeing from King Saul, the pursuers searched the "Crags of the Ibex" in the vicinity of Ein Gedi. In a cave near here, David cut off the corner of Saul's robe.

BIBLE REFERENCES

Area was occupied by the Amorites (Genesis 14:7)
Here David took refuge in a cave and cut off a piece of Saul's robe (I Samuel 23:29-24:22)
The Acacia tree, from which the Ark of the Covenant was made, grows in this area (Exodus 25:5, 10, 13, 23)

THE DEAD SEA

The high salt content of the Dead Sea allows you to float on the surface. In addition to high salt, there is a high mineral content including bromide, magnesium and potash. Mud from the Dead Sea also has several therapeutic properties, including treating psoriasis and rheumatic disorders.

CONCLUSION OF DAY 6

We arrive back in Jerusalem late this afternoon and you probably should begin getting your things together since we will be checking out of our hotel in the morning (this applies to groups flying Lufthansa or British Air only). We will gather together for our last supper in Jerusalem this evening. Just reflect back over how much we have seen and experienced in these few days? Is it really time to go home? Well, not just yet, because we have a great day still to come!

NOTES

DAY 7

THE GARDEN TOMB

A few minutes after we depart the hotel we will arrive at a site just north from the Damascus Gate outside the Old City known as Skull Hill and Gordon's Calvary. This acre of land is controlled today by the Garden Tomb Association and was purchased by the British organization in 1893. This special place fulfills all biblical requirements as to the validity of the location where Jesus suffered, died, was buried and arose after three days and nights. Our tour of this special place will be led by a member of the association, usually a British minister or businessman on sabbatical.

This is one of the most exciting places we will visit during these days, for here we will focus on the location of Calvary and the empty tomb, as well as the atoning work of the sacrifice of our Lord and the proof of its acceptance, the resurrection! We know the Romans crucified at major intersections and on ground level, not on a hill as the famous hymn suggests! Outside the Damascus Gate, at a very busy intersection of Jaffa Road and the road to Damascus, is a place that qualifies as Skull Hill. The Roman writer Quintillion in his *Declarations* clearly indicated the purpose of doing so; "Wherever we crucify criminals, very crowded highways are chosen so that many may see it, and many may be moved by fear of it." In 1956 an Arab bus station was built at the base of the hill and today we must contend with noise and fumes. However, we can clearly see the skull and nearby is the garden with the tomb of a rich man!

We knew before we came the tomb was empty! We know it because we have experienced the risen Lord Jesus in our lives. But what a joy to enter this tomb and see the place where Jesus was laid and know that nothing could keep Him in the grave for He Lives! We will tour the garden and then have a special time of sharing.

BIBLE REFERENCES
Here Jesus was crucified and resurrected (Matthew 27:32-56, John 19:16-37)

EIN-KAREM

As we depart Jerusalem, to the west we will pass the village of Ein -Karem, the birthplace of John the Baptizer. Today, there are several educational institutions in the village and the Hadassah Hospital is very near.

EMMAUS

About a mile from Latrun and 15 miles west of Jerusalem on the 48 corridor lies the remains of ancient Emmaus. This is the place where Jesus appeared to the two travelers after His resurrection. Today, we view the remains of an early Byzantine Crusader church.

BIBLE REFERENCES

Here Jesus appeared to two disciples (Luke 24:13-35)

VALLEY OF ELAH

Our last stop before arriving at the Ben Gurion International Airport is the Valley of Elah. Here we will stop along the side of the highway at a dry riverbed, and we remember the story of David and Goliath. For it was in this valley where the army of Saul drew the battle lines. They were camped on one hill and the Philistines opposite them between Socoh and Azekah.

BIBLE REFERENCES

David slays Goliath (I Samuel 17:1-58)

NOTES

CONCLUSION

Can you believe it? A few days ago we began our "Trip of a Life- time" and now it draws to a close! I know you will agree this has been a life-changing experience! Think of the new friends you have made, both among our group and in Israel as well. Aren't you glad you made the sacrifice necessary to make this journey? I know right about now you are overwhelmed with all you have seen and heard these days, but I want you to know you have absorbed more than you think you have. After you return home, as you sit down with your Bible and your notes, things will come to you that you did not think you would re-member. I know it is true. Thousands have told me so. May His blessings be upon you as you become an Ambassador for His land!

Shalom and Next Year in Jerusalem!

RESOURCES

Many hours of study and research have gone into the preparation of this study and reference manual. The following resources were used and are recommended for further research:

Amman, Moshe, ed. *Carta's Historical Atlas of Israel*. Jerusalem: Carta.

Ben-Dov, Meir; Mordechai Naor; Zeev Aner. *The Western Wall*. Israel: Ministry of Defense Publishing House, 1983.

Berrett, LeMar C. *Discovering the World of the Bible*. Nashville: Thomas Nelson, 1979 (out of publication).

Dimont, Max I. *Jews, God and History*. New York: Mentor, 1994.

Friedman, Thomas. *From Beirut to Jerusalem*. London: Fontana, 1990.

Fruchtenbaum, Arnold G. *The Footsteps of the Messiah*. Tustin, California: Ariel Press, 1982.

Harris, Ralph W. *Dan to Beer-Sheba*. Springfield, Missouri: Empire Printing, 1979.

Ice, Thomas; Price, Randall. *Ready to Rebuild*. Eugene, Oregon: Harvest House, 1992.

Lambert, Lance. *Battle for Israel*. Eastbourne, East Sussex: Kingsway Publications, Ltd., 1975 (out of publication).

Ludwig, Charles. *At the Tomb*. Anderson, Indiana: Warner Press, 1991.

Mansfield, Peter. *A History of the Middle East*. New York: Penguin, 1991.

Reagan, David. *The Master Plan*. Eugene, Oregon: Harvest House, 1993.

The Holy Bible, New International Version. Grand Rapids: Zondervan, 1978.

Trever, John C. *The Dead Sea Scrolls: A Personal Account*. Grand Rapids: William B. Eerdmans, 1979.

Whiston, William, ed. *Josephus' Complete Works*. Grand Rapids: Kregel Publications, 1960-1983.

White, Rev. Bill. *A Special Place: "The Story of the Garden Tomb, Jerusalem"*. Lincolnshire: The Stanborough Press Limited, 1989.

Williamson, G. A., ed. *Josephus — The Jewish War*. New York: Viking Penguin, 1985.

Woods, Guy N. *Biblical Backgrounds of the Troubled Middle East*. Nashville: Gospel Advocate Co., 1991.

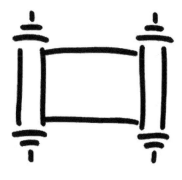

WORSHIP

AMAZING GRACE

Amazing grace! How sweet the sound
That saved a wretch like me!
I once was lost, but now am found;
Was blind, but now I see.

'Twas grace that taught my heart to fear,
And grace my fears relieved;
How precious did that grace appear
The hour I first believed.

Through many dangers, toils and snares,
I have already come;
'Tis grace hath brought me safe thus far,
And grace will lead me home.

The Lord has promised good to me,
His Word my hope secures;
He will my Shield and Portion be,
As long as life endures.

The earth shall soon dissolve like snow,
The sun forbear to shine;
But God, who called me here below,
Will be forever mine.

When we've been there ten thousand years,
Bright shining as the sun,
We've no less days to sing God's praise
Than when we'd first begun.

GREAT IS THY FAITHFULNESS

Great is thy faithfulness, O God my Father;
there is no shadow of turning with thee;
thou changest not, thy compassions, they fail not;
as thou hast been thou forever will be.

Great is thy faithfulness! Great is thy faithfulness!
Morning by morning new mercies I see;
all I have needed thy hand hath provided;
great is thy faithfulness, Lord, unto me!

Summer and winter and springtime and harvest,
sun, moon and stars in their courses above
join with all nature in manifold witness
to thy great faithfulness, mercy and love. [Refrain]

Pardon for sin and a peace that endureth
thy own dear presence to cheer and to guide;
strength for today and bright hope for tomorrow,
blessings all mine, with ten thousand beside! [Refrain]

HOLY, HOLY, HOLY! LORD GOD ALMIGHTY

Holy, holy, holy! Lord God Almighty!
Early in the morning our song shall rise to thee;
holy, holy, holy! merciful and mighty,
God in three persons, blessed Trinity!

Holy, holy, holy! All the saints adore thee,
casting down their golden crowns around the glassy sea;
cherubim and seraphim falling down before thee,
who wert and art and evermore shalt be.

Holy, holy, holy! Though the darkness hide thee,
though the eye made blind by sin thy glory may not see,
only thou art holy; there is none beside thee,
perfect in power, in love, and purity.

Holy, holy, holy! Lord God Almighty!
All thy works shall praise thy name, in earth and sky and sea;
holy, holy, holy! merciful and mighty,
God in three persons, blessed Trinity!

HOW GREAT THOU ART

O Lord, my God, when I in awesome wonder
consider all the works thy hand hath made,
I see the stars, I hear the mighty thunder,
thy power throughout the universe displayed;

Then sings my soul, my Savior God, to thee:
how great thou art, how great thou art!
Then sings my soul, my Savior God, to thee:
how great thou art, how great thou art!

When through the woods and forest glades I wander,
I hear the birds sing sweetly in the trees;
when I look down from lofty mountain grandeur
and hear the brook and feel the gentle breeze; [Refrain]

But when I think that God, his Son not sparing,
sent him to die, I scarce can take it in,
that on the cross, my burden gladly bearing,
he bled and died to take away my sin; [Refrain]

When Christ shall come, with shout of acclamation,
and take me home, what joy shall fill my heart!
Then I shall bow in humble adoration
and there proclaim, "My God, how great thou art!" [Refrain]

HIS NAME IS WONDERFUL

His Name is Wonderful
His Name is Wonderful
His Name is Wonderful
Jesus My Lord

He is the Mighty King
Master of everything
His Name is Wonderful
Jesus My Lord

He's the Great shepherd
The Rock of All Ages
Almighty God is He

Bow down before Him
Love and adore Him
His Name is Wonderful
Jesus My Lord

CROWN HIM WITH MANY CROWNS

Crown him with many crowns, the Lamb upon his throne.
Hark! how the heavenly anthem drowns all music but its own.
Awake, my soul, and sing of him who died for thee,
and hail him as thy matchless king through all eternity.

Crown him the Lord of life, who triumphed o'er the grave,
and rose victorious in the strife for those he came to save;
his glories now we sing who died and rose on high,
who died eternal life to bring, and lives that death may die.

Crown him the Lord of love; behold his hands and side,
rich wounds, yet visible above, in beauty glorified;
no angels in the sky can fully bear that sight,
but downward bends their burning eye at mysteries so bright.

Crown him the Lord of years, the potentate of time,
creator of the rolling spheres, ineffably sublime.
All hail, Redeemer, hail! for thou hast died for me;
thy praise shall never, never fail throughout eternity.

PSALM 23

A psalm of David.

1 The Lord is my shepherd, I shall not be in want.
2 He makes me lie down in green pastures,
      he leads me beside quiet waters,
3 he restores my soul.
      He guides me in paths of righteousness
      for his name's sake.
4 Even though I walk
      through the valley of the shadow of death,
      I will fear no evil,
      for you are with me;
      your rod and your staff,
      they comfort me.
5 You prepare a table before me
      in the presence of my enemies.
      You anoint my head with oil;
      my cup overflows.
6 Surely goodness and love will follow me
      all the days of my life,
      and I will dwell in the house of the Lord forever.

PSALM 100

A psalm. For giving thanks.

1 Shout for joy to the LORD, all the earth.
2 Worship the LORD with gladness;
    come before him with joyful songs.
3 Know that the LORD is God.
    It is he who made us, and we are his;
    we are his people, the sheep of his pasture.
4 Enter his gates with thanksgiving
    and his courts with praise;
    give thanks to him and praise his name.
5 For the LORD is good and his love endures forever;
    his faithfulness continues through all generations.

PSALM 67

1 May God be gracious to us and bless us
    and make his face shine upon us,
2 that your ways may be known on earth,
    your salvation among all nations.
3 May the peoples praise you, O God;
    may all the peoples praise you.
4 May the nations be glad and sing for joy,
    for you rule the peoples justly
    and guide the nations of the earth.
5 May the peoples praise you, O God;
    may all the peoples praise you.
6 Then the land will yield its harvest,
    and God, our God, will bless us.
7 God will bless us,
    and all the ends of the earth will fear him.

PSALM 117

1 Praise the LORD, all you nations;
    extol him, all you peoples.
2 For great is his love toward us,
    and the faithfulness of the LORD endures forever.

Praise the LORD.

NOTES

DISCOVERY CRUISES AND TOURS
www.discoverycruisesandtours.com

We are pleased to offer additional pastor-led,
quality, Bible-oriented tours.

The Journeys of Paul

We invite you to join us on an exciting journey to magnificent Greece and Turkey. We will tour Thessaloniki, Philippi, Delphi, Corinth and other historic Biblical sites. We will tour Athens and the spectacular Greek Isles, including the Isle of Patmos where John was in exile and received Revelation. We will stop in Turkey and tour Ephesus—a true archaeological wonder with deep Biblical significance. We will return home with a new understanding of Paul's outreach to the Greeks and subsequently to the world. Come join us for an amazing journey.

Biblelands Cruises

Biblelands Cruises provide a great opportunity to be at home for 7 to 9 nights aboard your deluxe ship sailing to exciting, Bible sites where you will be informed and challenged in your spiritual growth. Each cruise is hosted by Host pastor who will be sharing Biblical insights on location. Days at sea allow ample time to relax and renew your body as well as your soul.

OTHER RESOURCES BY GARY FRAZIER

HELL IS FOR REAL: WHY IT MATTERS

For many people, Hell is an outdated myth of ancient, uneducated people. However, the Bible is filled with many references describing Hell as a very real place and a very real destiny of those who do not have faith. Do you know where you will spend eternity? Explore what the Bible says about this important topic.

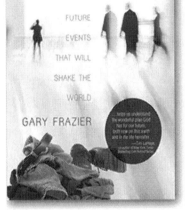

IT COULD HAPPEN TOMORROW: FUTURE EVENTS THAT WILL SHAKE THE WORLD

Are we living in the last days? Current events indicate that Old and New Testament prophecies are being fulfilled. Dr. Gary Frazier, a top prophecy scholar, pastor, speaker and author, identifies key indicators along with Biblical references that explain the demise of America, the coming Islamic invasion of Israel, nuclear weapons in Iran, and more.

MIRACLE OF ISRAEL

Everyone is looking for a miracle.
Families devastated by a faltering
economy. A college student facing the
horrific diagnosis of cancer. Corpo-
rately, whole nations are teetering on
the brink of despair and chaos. The
Miracle of Israel is a stunning exami-
nation of the millennia-old love that
God has for His people that:

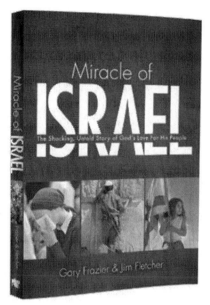

- Clearly conveys the promise God
  gave to Abraham
- Examines the ancient prophecies
  regarding Israel that have happened and are unfolding even
  today
- Provides an easy-to-read timeline of miracle after miracle related to
  the nation of Israel

Tracing the history of the Jewish people to the present day, the au-
thors look at prophecy after prophecy that clearly attest to the Lord's
miraculous promises. From historical records to personal, dramatic
stories, the *Miracle of Israel* shows us that, in keeping epic promises to
the nation of Israel, God's provision for each of us is sure, perfect, and
on time, every time.

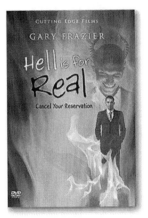

HELL IS FOR REAL: CANCEL YOUR RESERVARTION (DVD)

When I walked out of the theater after watching 'Heaven Is For Real', I felt uncomfortable, for the almost subliminal message was that, eventually, all people go to Heaven. Since the movie did not show the Biblical road to Heaven, it leaves a message that all people will go there.

IT COULD HAPPEN TOMORROW: FUTURE EVENTS THAT WILL SHAKE THE WORLD (DVD Series)

Are we living in the last days? Current events indicate that Old and New Testament prophecies are being fulfilled. Dr. Gary Frazier, a top prophecy scholar, pastor, speaker and author, identifies key indicators along with Biblical references that explain the demise of America, the coming Islamic invasion of Israel, nuclear weapons in Iran, and more.

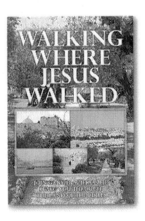

WALKING WHERE JESUS WALKED (DVD Series)

Join Gary Frazier as he leads through the land of the Bible.

BOOK GARY FRAZIER

To schedule speaking engagements with Gary Frazier, please contact him at **email@garyfrazier.com**. Additional teaching materials may be obtained online at **www.garyfrazier.com** or by phone at **817-595-2700**.

More copies of this book are available on Amazon.com
or contact:
IsraelTourBook@yahoo.com